A GLOW IN THE DARK:
Essays on Rizal

Cover Design by Raymund Ll. Liongson

A Glow in the Dark:
Essays on Rizal

Edited by
Serafin P. Colmenares, Jr.
Raymund Ll. Liongson

The Knights of Rizal
Aloha Chapter
Honolulu, Hawaii

A Glow in the Dark:
Essays on Rizal

Copyright © 2020

KDP ISBN: 9798682632718

Recommended entry:

Colmenares, Serafin P. and Liongson, Raymund Ll. (Eds.)
A Glow in the Dark: Essays on Rizal
Honolulu, Hawaii: The Knights of Rizal-Aloha Chapter, © 2020.

AUTHOR | Essays on Rizal

TABLE OF CONTENTS

PART III: RIZAL AND SOCIETY

FOREWORD

I MUST FORTHWITH congratulate the Aloha Chapter of the Knights of Rizal, headed by its Commander, Sir Dr. Serafin "Jun" Colmenares, Jr., KGCR, for its initiative in coming out with an e-Book with the fascinating title, *A Glow in the Dark: Essays* **on** *Rizal*. This electronic book edited by Sir Jun and Sir Dr. Raymund Liongson, KGCR is the first of its kind ever.

The "glow in the dark" has profound significance. For one, the essays and speeches embodied therein are a brilliant light that provides the reader a vivid glimpse into the life, ideas, ideals, virtues, hopes, aspirations and dreams of Rizal. Foremost, however, they show to us that Rizal was a "light of the world" which, in the Gospel according to St. Matthew (5:14-16), "gives light to all in the house" and so "shine(s) before others, that they may see (his) good deeds and glorify (the) Heavenly Father."

Truly, Rizal was (and is) that light for the Filipinos for them to free themselves from the slavery of colonialism and the bondage of ignorance, poverty, fear, hopelessness, and division. That light was oiled by his blood in martyrdom at an early age of 35, just a little older than Jesus Christ when He was crucified for the salvation and redemption of His people. Rizal's light would never dim. It will always be kept aglow in the hearts and minds of the Filipino people and even by humanity itself. The darkness cannot overcome it.

The "glow in the dark" insightfully places Rizal in a pedestal so that as a light he will forever guide the Filipino people in their journey toward the uncertain and even incomprehensible future and in the process make our country truly great in the community of nations. Rizal will make this COVID-19 pandemic a singular opportunity for the Filipinos to prove that they are with him in the frontline as an accomplished physician whose love of country is unmatched. To him, love of country "is the greatest, the most heroic and the most disinterested" of all loves because "it carries with it a divine stamp which renders it eternal and imperishable."

NON OMNIS MORIAR.

HILARIO G. DAVIDE, JR.
Former Chief Justice of the Philippine Supreme Court
Supreme Commander Emeritus, Knights of Rizal

9 June 2020.

PREFACE

Dr. José P. Rizal was a multi-talented, multi-dimensional genius. A Renaissance man, he epitomizes the height of Filipino achievement and exemplifies the idea that "genius knows no country." This volume is a modest attempt by the editors, and the officers and members of the Knights of Rizal-Aloha Chapter, to contribute to a greater understanding of the multi-faceted life as well as the ideas and teachings of the Philippines' foremost hero.

Written by academicians, members of the Knights of Rizal, and other Rizalian enthusiasts, the contents of this book are a collection of speeches and presentations given at various Rizalian events as well as essays that relate to the life, works, and teachings of Dr. Rizal. The articles are thematically organized around who he is and how his teachings and ideals impact education and society.

The book is divided into three parts. Part I includes articles that may shed more light about his life, allowing us to discover or rediscover him as a human being, a hero, and a martyr.

Part II comprises of articles around Dr. Rizal's influence on education and how contemporary instruction and learning interpret his works.

Part III includes essays on Dr. Rizal and how his works and teachings are impacting society – from the social and political dimensions of life to the philosophical and spiritual realms of our existence.

It is our hope that this volume will instill added interest and further study of Dr. Jose P. Rizal's life and works.

The editors would like to express their gratitude to all the contributors who freely gave their precious time to make this book possible. Our sincere thanks go to Amazon Kindle for publishing this e-book. Our heartfelt gratitude also goes to our families, especially our wives, for their patience, love, and support, and for understanding why we wanted to produce this book. Finally, to all who gave us support, financial or otherwise, in making this project possible, mahalo and aloha!

SERAFIN P. COLMENARES, JR.
RAYMUND LL. LIONGSON
Editors

INTRODUCTION

BY THE "AGE OF DISCOVERY" – at least from the standpoint of the European colonizers – the peoples of a Malay archipelago, later earning the moniker "the Pearl of the Orient," were living in societies that were witnessing the dawn of their early civilization. With their own social structures, customs and traditions, languages and writing systems, they were on their way toward shaping and developing their indigenous cultures and identities.

Then came the bearers of the sword and the cross, converting the natives into a dutiful population. In 1521, the islands were uncovered before Western eyes and the lust to subjugate its people and claim the lands was conceived. In 1543, the archipelago was named **Las Islas Filipinas** in honor of Philip II of Spain. In 1565, the first Hispanic settlement in the archipelago was established, and the country became part of the Spanish Empire which lasted for more than 300 years. This colonial period marked the Dark Era across the archipelago beset by abuse and exploitation, carnage and oppression, fear and submission. Human dignity was denied of the natives, derogatorily called Indios. Freedoms were curtailed and human rights and privileges were afforded only to the foreign masters and the agents of the church – the friars and the clergy. The flame that offered promise and hope to a people was snuffed out … and darkness fell. Fear and silence reigned, muting the people's sighs and wails. Raw courage and spirit were shackled with brutality and doused with blood, ending and concealing the will to be free. And darkness turned darker.

But in the darkness of the night was a glow that refused to surrender its light – Dr. Jose P. Rizal. Insisting that reason is more powerful than any material weapon, he used the pen and the creativity of the mind as primary tools to claim freedom and justice. Discarding the sword, he employed the power of character and words.

In his two novels that are now considered classic readings on reform and social change – *Noli Me Tangere* and *El Filibusterismo* – and other writings, Rizal unveiled the oppressive condition of his people in the hands of foreign colonizers. He also explored models of social change – from peaceful reforms to the more radical and forceful revolution. In the process, he accurately and beautifully captured the customs and tradition, traits and qualities of a people gravely mistreated by foreign iron hands with the help of local forces who coveted position and power in the repressive system.

But he went beyond wielding his pen. He organized communities, stood up and spoke out, listened and taught. In the halls of the elite, on exile or behind bars, he brought light in the minds of those dimmed by bigotry and power.

Dr. Rizal was an artist and a scientist, a social critic and an agent of change. He sparked the flint that ignited the consciousness of his people, bringing them together to fight for their freedom. He was a glow in the dark and now a source of hope whenever despair sinks in.

This is what this book is about. *A Glow in the Dark: Essays on Rizal* is a collection of speeches and essays on Rizal that we hope would rekindle our sense of history, struggle, and identity. It revisits the life of the martyr and hero and examines his enduring ideals and teachings. And as we get through the first quarter of the 21st century, many of the issues during Rizal's time such as poverty, socio-economic inequities, bureaucratic excesses, human rights abuse, and ignorance and bigotry, among others, continue to hold the country in darkness. Can the glow in the dark offer it hope?

RAYMUND LLANES LIONGSON

Part I
(Re)discovering Rizal

> **In order to know Rizal, one has to read Rizal.**

Ambeth Ocampo
Rizalian scholar
Philippine Daily Inquirer, June 15, 2018

Rizal: Frequently Cited But Seldom Read and Deeply Studied

Sir Elihu A. Ybañez, LL.B., KGCR

MAGANDANG GABI sa inyong lahat! It is a pleasure to join you, fellow knights, ladies, and gentlemen, in this celebration. I thank our special guests, for gracing this occasion.

Dr. Jose P. Rizal excelled in nearly everything that he did.[1] He even died well[2] – he refused to be blindfolded, he went to the execution ground with a peaceful countenance and normal vital signs, and even at the moment of his fall, Rizal turned his body so that he would end up lying on his back with his face to the sun. His last words were those of Jesus Christ: *consummatum est* - it is finished.[3] Rizal was not just a man of mind-boggling talent and world-class intellect; he was a nation builder. He depicted a great love for God, when in one of his last writings, Rizal expressed his eagerness to go to a place where there are no oppressors or executioners and where the One who reigns is God.[4] Mabini, in his memoir, remembered Rizal's agony: *"From the day Rizal understood the misfortunes of his native land and decided to work to redress them, his vivid imagination never ceased to picture to him at every moment of his life*

---

[1]Severino, Howie. "Why we love Rizal". gmanetwork.com/news/opinion/content/288259/why-we-love-rizal/story/ [Date Accessed: August 21, 2018].

[2]*Ibid.*

[3]Del Rio, Riz. "The Execution of a Hero: Dr. Jose Rizal". Slideshare.net

[4]Roces, Alejandro R. "Remembering Rizal". philstar.com. https://www.philstar.com/opinion/2007/12/29/35714/remembering-rizal [Date Accessed: Accessed: August 21, 2018].

the terrors of the death that awaited him... The life of Rizal, from the time he dedicated it to the service of his native land, was therefore a continuing death, bravely endured until the end for love of his countrymen."[5]

We are blessed to have a hero like Dr. Jose P. Rizal whose life and martyrdom continue to inspire and move Filipinos to fight for their rights as a people through non-violent means and to value education as the means to obtain equality, freedom, and justice.[6] Jose Rizal has likewise won his cherished place in the heart of the world. Rizal's courageous assertion of Filipino dignity and love of liberty was one of the first cries of nationalism in the world. Many were struck by Rizal's universal message of emancipation and upright leadership. Many are still captivated by his ideals despite differences in distance, culture, and time.

Despite all these, not many know Rizal by actually reading his writings. Rizal is cited all the time, but seldom read and deeply studied. For instance, many do not know that Jose Rizal authored an unfinished third novel, a sequel to *El Filibusterismo,* entitled *Makamisa,* which means after mass in English.[7] Very few scholars have actually read his entire body of work. Apart from Ambeth Ocampo and other historians like Teodoro Agoncillo, no one can say that they truly know Dr. Jose P. Rizal.[8]

May this joyous occasion be an opportunity to celebrate the great man that Rizal was and to draw inspiration from one of the first citizens of the world whose sublime faith in God and burning idealism are what we hope to see reawakened in the world today. More importantly, may we

---

[5]Ibid.

[6]Ibid.

[7]Perez, Ernesto C. "Jose P. Rizal at 150". realttorney.com. http://www.realttorney.com/2011/06/18/jose-p-rizal-at-150/ [Date Accessed: August 21, 2018].

[8]Ibid.

be prompted to read more about him and his works because in doing so, we would not only get to know Rizal more but we would understand ourselves better. If we realize, for example, how Rizal rose from his limitations and became what we know of him today, then we can rise from our weaknesses and challenges to become the people and leaders we should be.[9] We would likewise be in a better position to explain to the youth Rizal's relevance and how his novels are sad reflections of the present Philippines still.

This affair is likewise an appropriate time to enhance our relations and fellowship, and to take our solidarity to the next level. We unite because we know that we are better and stronger together. Let us carry out meaningful projects and be serious with the Order's mission, but let us not forget to have fun and enjoy camaraderie along the way. In addition, we give recognition to whom it is due. Highlighting achievements and acknowledging contributions are key factors in establishing a positive organizational culture. Our goal is not just to seed social change, but we also aim to provide value to our brother knights and advocates that they cannot find anywhere else.

In this gathering, let us be reminded that in order to do our work of propagating Rizal's teachings effectively, we need to keep our own house in order. This means conducting ourselves in accordance with the principles of Dr. Jose P. Rizal, treating our fellow knights with respect and fidelity, maximizing our impact by planning carefully and stewarding our resources wisely, and looking after the long-term health of the Order by ensuring that both our leadership and membership are strong and engaged. Everybody should get to have that feeling – the passion and conviction for and connection to the noble work the Order is doing. Let us continue to be exemplars of Rizalian values and illustrious vanguards of Rizal's legacy and heritage in both our individual and corporate capacities.

---

[9]Ibid.

THE HUMAN SIDE OF DR. JOSE P. RIZAL

Belinda A. Aquino, PhD

Introduction

FOR THE PAST hundred thirty years, Jose P. Rizal has been the national hero of the Philippines following his execution by the Spanish colonial regime for actively "fomenting" the Philippine Revolution of 1896, which marked the final downfall of the regime that had been in power for more than three centuries.

Martyr, nationalist, medical doctor, artist and author of two monumental novels, *Noli Me Tangere* (Social Cancer) and *El Filibusterismo* (The Subversion), which were the two most influential novels in changing the course of Philippine history in the 18th and 19th centuries. With his tireless energy as a writer of numerous articles, manifestos, essays and other writings, which were circulated worldwide, Rizal embodied the very qualities of leadership and commitment needed to undermine and finally end the Spanish regime in the Philippines.

Because of his martyrdom in choosing to sacrifice his own life to defend the Filipino struggle for freedom, Rizal has been immortalized in the annals of Philippine history. In the words of one of his early biographers and translators, Jorge Bocobo, Rizal was the unending beacon of the Filipino soul, whose martyrdom "rebukes oppression, avarice, intolerance, inferiority complex and subserviency (sic), and exalts righteousness, patriotism, abnegation, love of freedom, nationalism and civic virtue."[1]

---

[1] Bocobo, Jorge. El Filibusterismo. Translated from the original in Spanish to English. Manila, Philippines, 1957: iii.

Indeed, Rizal has been celebrated almost to the extreme by the country he left behind, holding him up on a pedestal as a "demigod" and a "saint"transcending humanity and mortality, and has been immortalized in numerous statues, sculptures, carvings and other symbols of historical greatness and significance in practically all the major cities and towns of the Philippines. His final resting place is the Luneta Park in the heart of Manila where he bravely faced his executioners who shot him with high-powered rifles on December 30, 1896.

At times the accolades and honors accorded him transcend the geographical and intellectual. From being called the "First Filipino," Rizal has been the embodiment of the "first Asian Nationalist and leading "Propagandista" in Europe in the 19th century.[2]

Even in a sleepy district called Kalihi Valley in Honolulu, there is a church which venerates him as a "saint" with his portrait posted on a wall for every parishioner, visitors and tourists to see. The founder of the church, Hilario Moncado, originally from the Philippines, established this place of worship in the name of the Filipino Federation of America. Moncado had also earlier "colonies" as places of worship in some places in the Visayas and Mindanao regions of the Philippines.

If Rizal were alive today, he himself would probably be astounded by the slew of superlatives and accolades heaped upon him since his martyrdom. Those who are left behind, especially the younger generations long after Rizal lived would probably ask, "Who was Jose Rizal?"; "Who was this extraordinary mortal who gave his life so that his country and people would live in freedom?"; "What was he really like as a human being?"

---

[2]Cullinane, Michael. *Ilustrado Politics: Filipino Elite Responses to American Rule*, 1898-1908. Quezon City, Philippines, 2003: 30.

This essay attempts to explore and dig deeper into the various dimensions of Rizal's life, particularly his participation in the fateful 1896 Philippine Revolution that put the country in a turbulent cycle of historical events marking similar struggles in Asia, Latin America, and Africa. Note that his execution at the young age of 35 inspired the first "nationalist revolution" in Asia in 1896, which established the first "democratic republic" that lasted until 1901, only to be colonized a second time – this time by the United States of America until 1946. According to another biographer of Rizal, Leon Ma. Guerrero, the Philippine success in freeing itself from Western colonialism inspired other examples in that region of the world only half a century after the execution of Rizal. (Guerrero 1961: xv). It is for this reason that Rizal is often called the "Pride of the Malay Race." Malay population encompasses a vast territory, particularly in Southeast Asia.

Historical Background

A summary of the highlights of Rizal's life and the notable milestones that catapulted him to national fame and significance is necessary to understand more deeply the essence of his humanity and character beyond the façade. His numerous achievements had made him attain the stature of *primus inter pares*, meaning "first among equals." Peers were his colleagues in the Propaganda Movement that Rizal and other intellectual and nationalists from the Philippines who had left their country and settled temporarily in Spain organized to call attention to their cause for the liberation of their country before Spain and other countries in Europe.

According to Regis Romero II, who had served as the Supreme Commander of the Order of the Knights of Rizal

---

[3]The Cavite Uprising of 1872 was sparked by the resistance of the three Filipino priests against the decision of the Spanish authorities to assign only Spanish priests to the parishes, thus depriving Filipino priests of their right to serve in the Philippines.

in the Philippines, it is obvious from the life of Rizal that he has been *destined for greatness* (emphasis added), but that his transformation was gradual (Romero 2003:107.)

Though Rizal was born to an upper middle-class family in Calamba in Laguna, a province south of Manila, he experienced personal difficulties early in life. His mother, Teodora Alonso y Realonda, was falsely accused of a crime that she did not commit by Spanish local authorities. She was forced to walk a long distance under a hot sun which had serious effects on her health afterwards. The incident embittered the young Rizal against the ruling class in his town that would intensify as he grew older and witnessed more examples of Spanish oppression.

The other major event that deeply enraged his sense of justice was the execution of three Filipino priests – Fathers Jose Burgos, Mariano Gomez and Jacinto Zamora – who were falsely accused of complicity in the so-called "Cavite Revolt of 1872" which broke out against the ruling Spaniards. The three priests were collectively known as "Gomburza," an acronym derived from their family names.[3] They were killed by a device called *garrote*, which strangled the priests until they were dead. Rizal was only eleven years old when he learned of this gruesome strangulation in the then Bagumbayan field, which was later the scene of his own execution in 1896.

Rizal would later dedicate his first novel, *Noli*, with the following message: "While we wait to clear your names someday, refusing a party to join your death, let these pages serve as a wreath of withered leaves on your forgotten graves." (Guerrero 1865: viii). And Rizal's dedication added: "Whoever attacks your memory without sufficient proof has blood upon his hands."

Such concern and manifestation of compassion and kindness to victims of injustice and violence would later characterize Rizal's own relationships with his peers and co-patriots in the longer struggle against Spain to obtain freedom for Filipinos.

Internal politics in the Propaganda Movement in Europe was bound to happen among propagandists. But Rizal, despite his prominent stature in the movement, again showed his compassionate and accommodating side. Romero narrates the 1891 meeting of the *Propagandistas* to elect the new officers of *La Solidaridad*, which was the organ of the Movement then headed by Marcelo H. del Pilar. When the election approached, the name of Jose Rizal was put forward to challenge del Pilar. This caused much tension among the Propagandistas who eventually took sides when the election was held.

According to Romero, the officers of the Movement lined up behind the two candidates. Pilar was supported by the following: Antonio Luna, Dominator Gomez, Salvador Vivencio del Rosario, Mariano Ponce, and Eduardo Lete. On the other side, Rizal was supported by Moises Salvador, Baldomero Roxas, Gregorio Aguilera, Lauro Dimayuga, Brigido Morado, Jose Abrera, and Jose Alejandrino (Romero 2018: 122).

The election resulted in a run-off because neither candidate had enough votes indicating a deadlock. One would think Rizal would have been more aggressive in pursuing the position had he been more inclined to accumulate power. But he did not and decided to be gracious enough to let del Pilar prevail. Rizal showed considerable humility and kindness on this issue.

Romero concludes: "Realizing that the exercise only divided them, Rizal decided to pull out of the race. He stuck to his decision even when on the third voting he won the election." (Romero: *ibid*) He was more concerned in preserving the unity that the group had developed since they launched the paper. (Romero: *ibid*). After all, the name of the movement's organ was *Solidaridad,* meaning solidarity.

This shows another instance where Rizal showed a great

deal of compassion and humility. He left afterwards for France to concentrate on his writing. He showed his capacity for self-sacrifice over the quest for power.

Rizal's Exile to Dapitan in Mindanao

As fate would have it, Rizal decided to return to the Philippines in1892 to resume his revolutionary activities. He immediately immersed himself in organizing the *La Liga Filipina* (the Philippine League). The purpose of his return to his homeland was obvious to the Spanish authorities: he wanted to resume his activities with the revolutionary movement among his compatriots in the Philippines. The revolutionary movement called *Katipunan* was in full swing, posing a continuing irritant to the Spaniards.

Rizal was arrested and exiled to Dapitan on the island of Mindanao. Not much is known about this particular phase in Rizal's troubled life. What did he do in this God-forsaken island which would be his place of exile for the four years immediately preceding his execution four years later in 1896?

His exile in Dapitan would be the equivalent of a "house arrest" in modern times. It is tantamount to a prison of sorts, although he was free to spend his exile provided he followed the conditions set up by Manila on how to spend his time. According to existing literature, he set up a medical clinic where he performed operations on the residents, particularly those with eye problems. He had training in ophthalmology when he lived in Europe. He was devoted to his companion, Josephine Bracken, who was reported to be his wife, although there was no confirmation of their relationship. But it was known that Bracken's uncle who travelled with her to Mindanao to be with Rizal, was being treated by Rizal for his health issues. He tended a garden and lived a quiet life.

Some scholars have wondered whether he had any contact with the Muslims in northern Mindanao who were at this time also engaged in a struggle to repel the invading Spaniards. But he had enough to do under the terms of his exile, and adding another struggle would have been a quixotic quest.

While he was in Dapitan, he received messages from the Katipunan members north of Manila to commit his support to the incipient revolution against the Spaniards. The Katipunan was a secret society organized by Andres Bonifacio to gain support from the masses to join the struggle. The conventional conclusion following this dialogue was that, Rizal cautioned against proceeding with the Revolution without sufficient arms and resources to defeat the Spaniards. He was being cautious and realistic.

Unfortunately, his message was misunderstood by the leadership of the Katipunan. Rizal was seen as being against the Revolution, which was not correct. All he commented on was the timing of the proposed uprising. He was not on the same wave length with his colleagues as far as the possibility of a successful revolution was concerned.

In a few months, he was allowed to return to Manila to defend himself in a trial for his reported complicity with the *Katipunan*. He was found guilty and thrown to prison in Fort Santiago where he was detained until it was time for his execution on December 30, 1896. It was the end of an era.

Analyzing Rizal in His Own Terms from his Two Novels

A deeper reading of Rizal's twin novels, the *Noli* and *Fili*, is expected to yield a richer consciousness into his basic character and essential humanity. He was, of course, immune from the controversies and misgivings that surround exceptional individuals who have reached a certain level of greatness.

Since we have only known Rizal in his writings and the various markers of his greatness and leadership in statues, sculptures, buildings, institutions and public symbols memorializing him, this effort to take a closer look may yield more insights into his inner persona that most of us had not been aware of before.

We will start from the *Noli* in which Rizal is portrayed as Crisostomo Ibarra, having just returned to the Philippines after spending seven years in Europe, notably Spain. The *Noli* is essentially the story of Ibarra and the sweetheart, Maria Clara, left behind during his lengthy sojourn abroad. He, of course, was still very much in love with her and they spent much of time together recalling their early happy childhood days. Ibarra could not wait to tell Maria the plans he had envisioned for their hometown of San Diego, such as establishing a "free and progressive school" for the younger generation. During the town fiesta, Ibarra gave a dinner in his house inviting many of the town's dignitaries including the Franciscan curate, Padre Damaso, who had persecuted Ibarra's father, Don Rafael Ibarra, and had him in jail for imagined "crimes" including not having gone to "confession" to Padre Damaso.

After learning the truth about his father's incarceration and death, Ibarra sets out to confront the offending priest who would not relent. In fact, the priest directed his anger against Ibarra himself calling him a "native" who had acquired a little education in Europe and became a "doctor." Upon hearing all these insults against his father and himself, Ibarra lost all civility and tried to strike Padre Damaso with a knife. As Bocobo describes the incident, "Ibarra seized a knife and stepped on the friar's neck. Padre Damaso tried to stand up but Ibarra seized him by the collar and held him down." Bocobo 1957: xxii).

The once pleasant and polite Ibarra had become an angry man ready to kill. He continued his invectives against the priest and screamed at the top of his voice, saying, "Priest of a God of peace, whose mouth is full of sanctity and religion but whose heart is full of meanness!" He turned into a raging bull, his knife-wielding arm ready to kill the friar "when Maria intervened and stopped the avenging arm."

(Bocobo 1957: xxiv)

Ibarra was excommunicated by the town's Archbishop and forbidden to set foot on the house of Capitan Tiago, Maria Clara's father. Padre Damaso in turn pressured Capitan Tiago to break off the engagement of Maria Clara to Ibarra. Maria was later forced to marry a man visiting from Europe, named Linares.

This episode in the *Noli* is just one example of Ibarra's complicated life which would end in his exile never to be seen by Maria Clara again. It mirrors the many difficulties and troubles in his real life which has been memorialized in various ways as cited earlier. It shows a different perspective of the man that we would never have imagined if we only focused on his greatness and achievements as a national hero. It makes him look like a human being – the other side of his celebrated persona which has been immortalized in history.

In the *Fili*, Rizal re-appears as Simoun, the Jeweler businessman, having morphed from Crisostomo Ibarra in the *Noli*. Compared to Ibarra, this reincarnation in the person of Simoun is a bitter and disillusioned idealist, who nevertheless continues his struggle against Spanish imperialism. He has become resentful of many of his peers in the revolutionary movement, and even with adherents from the younger generation typified by Basilio who was not at all averse to learning the Spanish language as a way to keep up with current developments in the struggle. Simoun is unmoved and gives a ringing sermon on the negative consequences of continuing Spanish tyrannical rule over the Philippines. He retorts:

"You ask for parity of rights, the Spanish way of life, and you don't realize that what you are asking is death, the destruction of your national identity, the disappearance of your homeland, the ratification of tyranny." (Guerrero 1965: 49).

He gets even more impassioned with his fellow nationalists

and intellectuals who had internalized their education under the Spanish as a form of "systematic obscurantism" which favors assimilation to a culture foreign from their own.

Continuing his diatribe, Simoun asks rhetorically, "What is to become of you? A people without a soul, a nation without freedom; everything in you will be borrowed, even your defects. You ask for Hispanization ... And if you were given that, what do you have to gain?" (Guerrero 1965: 49)

Simoun could not seem to contain his anger and disillusionment with his compatriots. He goes on and on with his fiery speech and ends with, "Resignation is not always a virtue; it is a crime when it encourages oppression. There are no tyrants where there are no slaves!" (Guerrero: *ibid*)

The last sentence has become a byword in studies analyzing the history of Philippine colonialism under foreign powers. It has been repeated time and again as a challenge to the Filipino people should there be future attempts to violate the nation's sovereignty, to what Spain and later America had done previously by force of arms.

Unlike the more soft-spoken Ibarra in *Noli*, the irrepressible Simoun was much more aggressive and relentless in pursuing and winning Philippine independence under all costs. If assimilation and peaceful evolution were the alternatives, these may never be realized and tyranny will prevail.

True to his literary soul, Rizal, through Simoun in *Fili*, employs a lot of rhetoric, metaphor, simile, hyperbole, ridicule, sarcasm, humor, laughter, caricature and other devices to describe the various characters in both the *Noli* and *Fili*. He reserves his most acerbic and cutting remarks for the friars whom he had condemned from the very start.

The chapter entitled "A Class in Physics" in *Fili* is a classic example of his ability to ridicule the Jesuit instructors in Physics, other sciences and fields of learning. Describing a Professor of Geography, for instance, Rizal says despite being a major in Geography, this teacher still doubts whether the world was round. He and other instructors seemed to be interested more to cover up their incompetence with a "science of religion." The narrative involving the "miseducation" of students by "uneducated" friar instructors is too long to summarize here but it is downright hilarious.

In the novel, Simoun becomes a fugitive once again because of his relentless revolutionary activities. He was shot in an encounter with the "guardia civil" (civil guards) who chased him till he disappeared in the shadows. Fortunately, he found shelter in a home by the sea owned by a Filipino priest named Father Florentino. The good father took care of Simoun who, while suffering badly from his wounds, was still talking about the need for a politics of defiance. And with it, the hope that the youth of tomorrow would carry on the struggle for Filipino freedom.

Father Florentino held Simoun's hand which had gotten cold. He knows Simoun was dead. The priest stretches his hand in the direction of the winds coming from the ocean. He says a brief prayer for Simoun: "Let Nature keep thee in the profound abyss among the corals and pearls of her eternal seas.... When for a sacred and sublime cause, men should need thee, God will know how to take thee out of the bosom of the waves..." (Bocobo 1957:359)

Conclusion

This essay has been a seminal attempt to explore the deeper facets of the life of Jose Rizal in hopes of finding certain meanings and nuances that go beyond the facade of his immortality composed of the numerous statues, sculptures, institutions, buildings, universities, schools, and other physical markers carrying his name as the national hero of the Philippines and a symbol of the country's ultimate pride and honor.

This analysis is not exhaustive by any means because Rizal's genius is unfathomable and his output of books, journals, monographs, articles, speeches, essays, art work, poems, paintings, manifestos, and other products of a superior intellect and prodigious work ethic was simply astounding. It will take a long time to exhaust the extent of his intellectual vitality, if that can be done at all. More research insights will certainly emerge as is the case with great events in history and our knowledge of Rizal will continue to be enriched.

His history and story have become ingrained in the nation's psyche and even when the words have faded from the books, Rizal's amazing life and spirit will remain. Such is the stuff of legend.

References

Aquino, Belinda A. "Rizal's Vision: To Build a Filipino Nation," in Raymund Llanes Liongson and Serafin P. Colmenares, Jr. (eds.). *Jose Rizal's Legacy and Nation-Building*. 2013: Honolulu: Order of the Knights of Rizal, pp. 8-14.

Cullinane, Michael. 2003. *Ilustrado Politics: Filipino Elite Responses to American Rule, 1898-1901*. Quezon City, Philippines: Ateneo de Manila University Press.

Mabini, Apolinario. 1931. *La Revolucion Filipino*. Manila: National Historical Commission. Translated into English by Leon Ma. Guerrero. 1969. Manila: National Historical Commission.

Romero, Regis, "In Every Filipino, A Rizal," in Liongson and Colmenares, 2013, pp. 15-23.

Rizal, Jose. 1886. *El Filibusterismo*, a Novel Translated into English by Soledad Lacson-Locsin. 1996. Honolulu: University of Hawaii Press.

Rizal, Jose. 1891. *Noli Me Tangere*, a Novel Translated into English by Leon Ma. Guerrero. 1961. Hong Kong: Longman Group, Ltd.

Rizal, Jose. 1891. *El Filibusterismo*, a Novel. Translated by Leon Ma. Guerrero. 1965. Hong Kong: Longman Group, Ltd.

Rizal, Jose. 1891. *El Filibusterismo* (Unexpurgated). Translated by Jorge Bocobo. 1957. Quezon City, Philippines: R. Martinez & Sons.

Reflections and Shadows: Revisiting Rizal

Sir Clement Bautista, KGOR

As we approach 123 years since José Rizal's death, the question of Rizal's relevance for contemporary society may again be revisited. Beyond the grand symbolism of Rizal's martyrdom that forever forms a pivotal moment in the Philippine's historical consciousness or, on a more personal level, how Rizal's prodigious talents and accomplishments humble the rest of us mortal Filipinos, we may still legitimately question the contemporary relevance of Rizal's wide-ranging writings – all of which reflect the ideas and sensibilities of the 19th century, an era before television, cell phones and online dating. In essence, what can we (still) learn from Rizal?

Re-discovering Rizal

In the Rizal@150 special issue of the journal, *Philippine Studies*, Ramon Guillermo poses several questions or dilemmas regarding Rizal's thinking on *Indio* intelligence and biological determinism. Guillermo does this by examining translations of Rizal's original Spanish texts in *El Filibusterismo* and in correspondence between Rizal and his life-long Austrian friend and mentor, Ferdinand Blumentritt. As a result of translators' conceptual clarifications or word choices, the Tagalog, German and English versions that have been passed down to us are what could be called, PC ('Philosophically Correct') translations in which some of the "bite" of the originals were toned down, redirected or removed entirely.

It is generally accepted by readers of Rizal that he believed the educational systems installed in the Philippines were part of a Spanish colonial indoctrination that bred a character and constitution which only *looked like* laziness but, in fact, was a rational response to colonial – especially cleric – domination. This argument was explicit in his essay, "The Indolence of the Filipino," published in 1890, a year before the *Fili*. So it would seem at this point, Rizal sided with the "nurturing" side of any Nature vs Nurture debate of how intelligence is created.

Examining the *Fili*, Guillermo focuses on the chapter, "A Class in Physics," where Rizal, as narrator, begins with the observation that in spite of our schooling, there are no great native *Indio* scientists. After pointing out the restricted use of scientific tools during classroom teaching, Rizal introduces a discussion or, rather, a disputation over the object and substance of a mirror. It is here that Guillermo points out a PC moment, where translators consistently "corrected" Rizal's use of "induccion" when referring to the scientific enterprise. This translating correction was, it seems, a way to distinguish more clearly scientific methods (deduction) from the philosophic (induction).

This dichotomy appears to make sense and simplifies (or eliminates) any further query into why Rizal really did use the term "induccion" for BOTH scientific and philosophic endeavors. As translated and as we are currently taught in school, science begins with observations (i.e., 'data') while philosophy starts from speculative abstractions (i.e., 'what ifs'), and both respectively draw generalizations from them – deductions for science and inductions for philosophy. Rizal's use of "induccion" for both forms of knowledge would seem to reflect an out-dated notion of epistemology...or does it? The tools and raw materials may differ, but the intellectual process fundamentally remains the same.

The chapter's extended disputation on the composition of a mirror not only illustrates professorial pedantry but highlights the phenomenological, if not also the ontological, structure of knowledge. To the distress of students, the physics professor continuously contradicts any answer a student might offer by provoking grammatical and referential confusion, while simultaneously shaming and demeaning each responding student. On one level, this class exercise is a prime example of an authoritarian educational environment and, yet, the distinction between a mirror's reflection and its substance is one worth dwelling on, especially if it relates to intelligence and heredity.

The contradictions contained in Rizal's story of the mirror are analogous to those reflected in the well-known fable of the cave in Plato's *Republic*. In this ancient fable, bound cave-dwellers are limited to experiencing people outside the cave as shadows projected upon the cave walls, such that their reality is restricted to the tactile and visual images of shadows. However, this limitation does not prevent them from creating their *own* reality based on their existence within the cave, no matter how different it might be from the reality of the outsiders. The contradiction presented here, like that of the Rizal's mirror narrative, is to ask, what is real? In this case, the shadows or the people producing the shadows? Of course, the answer is – both are real. In fact, a third reality exists: that of the narrator. Each exists in its own conceptual and experiential world.

"I'm Smarter Than You Are...It's In My Genes"

So, what does all this have to do with intelligence? Or heredity? Or inheritable intelligence?

As noted earlier, Rizal seems to side with the nurturing position of the Nature vs Nurture debate of intelligence. However, Guillermo digs up some Rizal-Blumentritt correspondence that, in the original Spanish, indicates Rizal does give Nature (or heredity) a nod:

> Concerning the *limited intelligence in races,* after a detailed study of the subject, I believe like you [Blumentritt] do, that there is and there is none. With regard to intelligence, it is like riches. There

are rich nations and poor nations; there are rich individuals and poor individuals. The rich who pretends to have been born rich is mistaken – he was born as poor and as naked as the child of a slave. What he has inherited is the *accumulated wealth of his ancestors.* I believe then that intelligence is inherited. Races which have been obliged to work with their brains on account of certain special conditions, have developed them more, then have transmitted them to their descendants who later have continued on, etc., etc. European nations are rich, but the present nations cannot say with temerity that they have been born rich. They needed centuries of struggle, wise combinations, liberty, laws, thinkers, etc. who bequeathed to them these riches. The intelligent races today are so after a long period of heredity. (Rizal to Blumentritt, 4 July 1895)

Rizal could be faulted for merely elaborating on the dominant evolution perspectives of the 19th century but, as Guillermo points out, Rizal seems to have adopted the "passing on of acquired traits" theory of Jean-Baptiste Lamarck over the more social evolutionary theories of Herbert Spencer in which inheritable *social* conditions shape intelligence. According to Lamarck, "a change in the environment causes changes in the needs of organisms living in that environment, which in turn causes changes in their behavior. Altered behavior leads to greater or lesser use of a given structure or organ; use would cause the structure to increase in size over several generations, whereas disuse would cause it to shrink or even disappear."

The notion that individuals can adapt to a physical or social environment and, then, mutate physiologically in response to their environment is generally no longer accepted in Western science. Yet, Rizal's view of nurturing depends on developing intelligence and, then, passing on that acquired intelligence (and, perhaps, other physiological mutations) through subsequent generations – as a "race." It is easy to imagine how this seemingly disinterested scientific theory becomes the justification for encouraging even more unseemly behavior and ideas.

Lest we forget, this biological transmission of intelligence was at the root of eugenic theories promulgated in the late 19th and early 20th centuries. An avowed eugenicist, Paul Popenoe, even promoted the idea that college-educated youth need to improve their social skills in order to have more children, thus increasing the overall intelligence of society. Other eugenic spin-offs ranged from the IQ testing movement (used to identify and rank "idiots," "imbeciles" and the "feebleminded") to the Nazi atrocities of WWII, both of which were intended to cleanse society of "undesirables."

One would like to believe Rizal's stomach would turn had he lived to witness these institutional, turn-of-the-century applications of eugenic theory. One would also like to believe discredited racist theories have disappeared from public discourse; unfortunately, they often remain simmering beneath the surface and periodically poke their heads up, cloaked in new rhetoric and branding.

The most conspicuous re-emergence of the eugenic/racist theory is the current MAGA ("Make America Great Again") movement of U.S. President Donald Trump. The particular brand of nationalism promoted by the Trump administration demonizes "outsiders" as well as "insiders" who look like or identify with "outsiders." For the Trump administration, nationalism is a scapegoating and cleansing movement where all the country's ills are a result from "outsiders" being among "us" (the imaged "high quality people").

A less offensive trend that, nonetheless, capitalizes on the public's ignorance of and desire for eugenics is the growing consumer market for DNA identification. Nowadays, on a trip to any drug store or pharmacy, you can often find a counter displaying products purporting to help "discover, map or reveal" your genetic heritage. While the most useful function for these products is to identify some genetic defect that was or can be passed on to future generations, the more common reason for consumers is to inquire into their own genetic heritage, i.e., who are your "blood relatives"? At least, that's the way these products are being advertised.

Whether it's for health ("be better"), beauty ("look better"), or identity ("find oneself"), the actual mechanisms in and purpose for DNA identification remain a mystery to most consumers. So much the better, for researchers Sheldon Krimsky and David Cay Johnston note that ancestry companies rely on statistical correlations to place consumers somewhere on an identity grid, and these statistics – short of surveying entire populations – are severely incomplete, resulting in false positives and false negatives. Moreover, correlations are based on existing and company-specific databases and, therefore, may differ depending on the database being used.

A much more common practice of associating "genes" with observable characteristics, including intelligence, is the totally discredited – but totally exploited – practice of physiognomy. Here, people's appearances (including their dress) are associated with certain desirable or undesirable characteristics. As unsound as physiognomy sounds, its use is pervasive: mass media (e.g., art, advertising and movie role casting), dating choices, and hiring (as much as we hope it didn't matter).

Returning to Rizal's story of the mirror and the separation of a mirror's substance from its reflecting surface, we can imagine in all these examples some form of eugenics propping up a particular trend or movement. Users or consumers interact with the genetics suppositions, but how they work and function is mostly hidden from users and consumers. They mostly see what they want to see – as reflections or shadows of themselves. Once this correlation is established, the potential for their exploitation is also set.

Where To Go From Here?

It has become fashionable in education and academic circles to criticize "the canon" which constitutes the basic readings buttressing our formal education. The usual criticism is that too much of the canon is represented by the works of "dead white men," and that our education would be "improved" with the addition of ideas and perspectives of non-dead, non-white, non-men, or some subset of it. If this criticism is valid, there might even be, as in the Philippines, a point at which we may exclude "dead brown men," too, if they are already in the canon. Rizal fits the bill – should he be excluded?

Except for religiously devout Rizalistas, most informed people consider José Rizal to be a man who had extraordinary intellectual gifts and was able to apply those gifts – including his martyrdom – to propel a revolutionary movement. Yet, he remains an intellectual of the 19th century, bounded by the very conditions, viewpoints and perspectives he helped to create. By returning to Rizal – flaws and all – we can still learn to appreciate the Philippines, as well as the world, on the brink of revolution.

The mix of science, philosophy, politics and art in Rizal's works is overwhelming. However, Rizal maintained a limited view of intelligence, one grounded in 19th century European thought. Today, the idea of multiple intelligences or creativities (Sternberg) better describes our differences in abilities and capabilities. Also, Rizal's understanding of genetic transmission was incomplete and flawed. Unfortunately for us, today, neither of these issues has disappeared from society – we still live in a world of reflections and shadows.

What I had hoped to illustrate in this essay was that it can be useful to go back to *a reading* of Rizal, listen to others and, then, to listen to oneself. Keep an open yet critical mind. At this point, once the dialog has been established, one can not only learn something *from* Rizal but also *through* him.

References

Citty, Clyde. 2008. "Eugenics, Race and Intelligence in Education." *British Journal of Educational Studies* 56(2): 228-231.

Guillermo, Ramon. 2011. The Problem of *Indio* Inferiority in Science: Rizal's Two Views. *Philippine Studies* (Historical and Ethnographic Viewpoints), 59(4): 471-493.

Krimsky, Sheldon and David Cay Johnston. 2017. *Ancestry DNS Testing and Privacy: A Consumer Guide*. Washington, D.C.: Council for Responsible Genetics.

Plato. 1968. *The Republic*. Translated by Allan Bloom. New York: Basic Books.

Popenoe, Paul. 1935. Education and Eugenics. *The Journal of Educational Sociology*, 8(8): 451-458.

Rizal, Jose. 1996 [1891]. "A Class in Physics" in *El Filibusterismo: Subversion*, pp. 98-108. Translated by Ma. Soledad Lacson-Locsin. Edited by Raul L. Locsin. Makati City, Philippines: Bookmark, Inc.

Rizal, Jose. 2011 [1890]. The Indolence of the Filipino, in *Jose Rizal: Political and Historical Writings*, pp. 227-265. Manila: National Historical Commission of the Philippines.

Spencer, Herbert. 1883. "The Primitive Man – Intellectual" in *The Principles of Sociology*, Volume 1, pp. 83-104. New York: D. Appleton and Company.

Sternberg, Robert J. 2001. What is the Common Thread of Creativity? *American Psychologist*, 56(4): 360-362.

Jean-Baptise Lamarck (1744-2919). http://www.ucmp.berkeley.edu/history/lamarck.html. (accessed 1/31/2019).

Jose Rizal: A Man For All Time

Virgie Chattergy, EdD

It is a privilege to be here with you to celebrate the life of a Filipino hero that you hold in high esteem. I have entitled this talk: Jose Rizal - A Man For All Time.

Everyone knows something about Jose Rizal. Tonight, I will share with you what I know and what I know revolves around two questions. The first question is "who is Jose Rizal?" What is he best known for, or how is he remembered? The second question is, "how do people react to him then and now?" And I will end with a question that you and I can think about beyond this evening and that is, "What lessons can we learn from Rizal and how he lived his life?"

The first question: who is Jose Rizal and for what is he best remembered?

Jose Rizal was a lover (aren't all Filipinos?). I don't mean by way of a Romeo, although a number of women found him very attractive and charismatic. To name a few, Josephine Bracken whom he married hours before he faced his executioners; a Segunda Katigbak, a Consuelo y Perez, a petite Gertrude Beckett, an Usui Seiko, and of course, the love of his life, Leonor Rivera. However, his relationship with these women is not what he is most remembered for. He had three loves in his life that surpassed all others: 1) his family, especially his mother; 2) his country; and 3) his love of learning. He was, to the end of his life, a devoted son; a loyal patriot and an outstanding scholar who had unquenchable thirst to learn. These three passions in his life permeated his actions. Let us explore how.

Mother and son were so close that she home schooled him when they kept him at home because at age six, he knew more than what the school in his village was able to teach.

Rizal took up medicine when he found out that his mother's eyes were failing and he wanted to take care of her. He dedicated a poem to her entitled "My First Inspiration" and I quote:

> "Why do the fragrant flowers
> exhale their sweet bouquet on this day?
> Why are sweet melodies heard
> like the sweet harmonies of singing nightingales?
> Why in grasses deep are carols heard
> as every bird leaps from stem to stem?
> Dear mother, in your praise –
> to greet you on your natal day…"

He wrote to his mother and wrote about her in his letters to his siblings, always reminding them to take care of her and their father.

Second, Rizal loved his country – passionately, undeniably and honorably.

In his famous poem, now known as "Mi Ultimo Adios" (My Last Farewell), he writes:

> "Fare thee well, motherland I adore,
> Pearl of the Orient Sea
> I go with gladness to give you my life…
> My dreams while still a child;
> my dreams in my youth
> Were to see you, gem of the Orient Sea,
> One happier day, your eyes
> Dried of tears, your smooth brow clear
> and free from the stains and the stigma of shame.
> God bless you – to die and to give you my life here,

under the sky expire
And in your mystic land, to sleep for eternity
Farewell to all I love - to die is but to rest."

He dedicated poems to his hometown, to the Filipino youth, to his mother tongue, to the virtues of work and his countrymen, wives, girls, boys. He was also a prolific letter writer. There is a book that talks about Rizal's hundred letters.

Rizal's third passion was his love of learning. His love of learning made him a consummate scholar. It is said that he read every book he could lay his hands on. And so he learned.

He learned by studying. He excelled in various fields of study: in the social sciences such as geography and history; in natural sciences such as chemistry, physics, metaphysics and cosmology; in the humanities such as languages, philosophy, poetry writing. He was without equal in his days as a student in the Philippines. He studied in Ateneo where he received first prize awards and excelled in almost every subject. He took advanced courses and completed his medical studies in the University of Santo Tomas, Philippines and Central University in Madrid, Spain.

He learned by traveling and his travels were extensive. He visited Italy, Spain Germany, Belgium, France, Switzerland, the U.S., and in Asia he visited Japan and Hong Kong. Furthermore, he learned the languages of these countries. He also learned Arabic, Hebrew and Latin.

He learned by teaching different subjects, even in Dapitan, while in exile.

He learned to be an artist. He enrolled in art classes taking up the art of painting, sketching and sculpture.

He learned anatomy and became a doctor, initially to help his mother but he also practiced medicine in Dapitan.

He learned by writing poetry and published his two famous novels that were used in part to accuse him of treachery and sedition: the *Noli Me Tangere* and *El Filibusterismo*. He wrote to expose the unjust laws and practices, to raise awareness and move his countrymen to bring about changes without violence. He used words and ideas to propose change. He used his mind without picking up arms to fight. He believed that the pen was mightier than the sword. Perhaps the time in which he lived was ripe for revolution, so his voice was muted. The time perhaps, was past for talking and deliberating. Or perhaps, he was ahead of his time. Jose Rizal was a reformer who advocated reform without violence.

We saw this same spirit emerge in Gandhi less than 50 years later. Regardless of which side of a conflict you support, Rizal's message is to act based on awareness and understanding and to appeal to reason. Rizal was gifted with a strong mind. He nurtured it, developed it and used it to make a difference in his world. A dynamic persona like that of Rizal, doesn't go unnoticed.

And so this realization led me to my second question. How do people react to him – then and now?

The answer is, it depends on which side of the fence one stands. Rizal was simple and complicated at the same time. He was candid and straightforward, but he was accused and suspected of deceitful acts. He was very well respected, but he was also criticized. He was admired, but he was also feared. He earned the loyalty of many, but he also gained enemies. He was charming, endearing, loving and loved, but he also provoked anger. How can one man bring out all these conflicting emotions? Rizal was obviously a fascinating man who will be written about for years to come.

My final question for all of us is to ask, "what lessons do we take away from his life and how he lived?" Some of these can be answered by Rizal's own words.

I will start with Rizal's own teachings and his writings because they are part of his legacy. They embody his message to us. Here are some thought provoking statements selected from his writings and letters:

- Exalt the mind through education. Education develops the body, heart, mind and soul. The schoolroom must be a scene of intellectual refreshment.

- To be informed leads to knowledge and knowledge is power

- Learning helps form character and instills good study habits.

- Education is the salvation of our country

- No reform is possible without education and liberty

- We are all human and can improve ourselves through education

- As you learn more, you gain confidence

Obviously, as an educator, I have selected his thoughts on the need for and the benefits of a good education. For education to flourish, it has to be supported and be allowed to open the minds to the larger world, he often said. In turn, education would create an even greater freedom of thought, for the individual and for the country. Ignorance, on the other hand, is a form of bondage. This was a radical thinking in his days, especially in the Philippines.

Finally, one cannot speak of Rizal without reference to his moral character. He was trustworthy in his dealings and relationship with women, friends and enemies alike. He was a law-abiding citizen who cautioned against breaking the laws. His message was always for fairness, for better and more representation in the Spanish Cortes. He encouraged kindness and compassion and cautioned against keeping company with persons of "bad habits". His insatiable curiosity, his perseverance, his determination and ability to focus on his goals are qualities that make Rizal a model and relevant to this day.

Perhaps, President Manuel Roxas' tribute to him in the 50th anniversary of Rizal's death captures the essence of the man:

> "Rizal's life was violently snuffed out by imperial minions who did not comprehend the eternal truth that man may be killed but ideas are indestructible.
>
> In the half-century since his death and still today, Rizal awakened our national consciousness more completely than any other figure in our history. We pay tribute to a long and swelling rank of heroes but Rizal towers over them all as he inspired all who came after him."

And this is why I say Jose Rizal is a Man For All Time.

Thank you.

Rizal, the Successful but Unhappy Pilgrim

Sir Serafin Colmenares Jr., PhD, KGCR

ONE MAJOR ASPECT of Rizal's life – in addition to his being a polymath, a Renaissance man, a man of various talents and accomplishments – was his being a traveler. He was the most travelled among Filipino heroes and was one of those who circumnavigated the world during his time. Rizal spent almost 24 years, or about 70% of his short 35-year-long life, traveling outside his hometown of Calamba. In addition to his domestic travels, Rizal went overseas, primarily Europe, three times. He passed and visited various countries and spent long periods in Spain, France and England. He also travelled to and lived for a short while in Japan and Hongkong, and even visited North Borneo (now Sabah).

Rizal had impressive travelogue, with many great things that come with it. But while his travels had given him much opportunities for self-development as well as tremendous productivity and achievements, Rizal saw himself deeply as a sad and unhappy pilgrim.

This presentation traces Rizal's life as a traveler and looks at his thoughts on travel as gleaned from his various writings which include his reminiscences, travel diaries and letters. His essay "On Travel" (*Los Viajes*), and his poem "Song of the Traveler" (*Canto del Viajero*) also tell something more about him. The latter is appended here for readers to see its poetic significance and meanings in Rizal's life.

Rizal's Travels

Rizal's first travel away from home was in June 1868 when, at the age of 7, he accompanied his father to Manila and Antipolo for a pilgrimage, via Cainta and Taytay. In June 1869, he was sent to Biñan for a private tutorship which ended in December 1870. He proceeded to Manila for his studies at Ateneo Municipal de Manila (1872-1877), where he obtained his Bachelor of Arts degree. He also matriculated at the Universidad de Santo Tomas from 1877 to 1882 for his medical studies, as well as his licentiate in surveying. He decided to leave the university, however, because of perception on racism and discriminatory practices by the school against *Indios*. Upon the urging of his brother Paciano and his uncle, but unknown to his parents, he went abroad to continue his medical studies.

First Travel Abroad

His first travel abroad was to Europe, where he stayed for five years and three months (1882-1887). He left Manila on May 3, 1882, passing by Singapore, Colombo, Ceylon (present day Sri Lanka), Aden (Yemen), Suez Canal and Port Said (Egypt), passing by Naples (Italy), then Marseilles (France) to Madrid (Spain) via Barcelona.

Rizal stayed in Madrid from 1882 to 1885, studying at the Universidad Central de Madrid for his medical studies. He also studied philosophy and letters. He likewise studied sculpting and painting at the Academy of Fine Arts in San Fernando, Madrid. In June 1884, he finished his medical course and became a licentiate in medicine. The following year, he finished all the courses for the degree of Doctor of Medicine. However, he did not submit his thesis as required for graduation, nor did he pay the fees. Thus, he was not awarded his degree. In June 1885, he received his licentiate in philosophy and letters.

After his studies in Spain, he travelled to France and Germany to specialize in ophthalmology. In Paris, he worked as a trainee under Dr. Louis de Wecker. He then travelled to Heidelberg, Germany, where he attended lectures and completed his eye specialization under Dr. Otto Becker at the University of Heidelberg Eye Hospital. He attended lectures at the University of Leipzig and befriended historian Prof. Friedrich Ratzel and anthropologist/ethnologist Dr. Hans Meyer. He went to Dresden, where he met Dr. Adolph Meyer, a naturalist from Dresden University. He then proceeded to Berlin where he stayed for more than six months, became a researcher at Real Biblioteca de Berlin and met Dr. Feodor Jagor and renowned pathologist Rudolph Virchow and his son Hans. It was in Berlin that he was able to publish his first novel, *Noli Me Tangere* (1887) with the help of Maximo Viola.

He left Berlin on May 11, 1887 for Teschen and Litomerice, Bohemia to meet his good friend Prof. Ferdinand Blumentritt. From Litomerice Rizal travelled to Prague to meet Dr. Wilkomm, natural history professor at the University of Prague-Brunn. He left on May 19, 1887 for Vienna where he stayed until May 25, 1887. From there he toured the River Danube, and proceeded to Salzburg, Munich, Nuremberg, Ulm, Stuttgart, Baden, Rheinfalls, and then to Switzerland, visiting Basel, Bern and Lausanne, staying in Geneva from June 3 to 23, 1887. Rizal proceeded to Italy where he visited Turin, Milan, Venice, Florence and Rome. Afterwards he went on to Marseille, France on his way back to Manila via Saigon.

Rizal returned to the Philippines despite warnings from friends and family due to the negative reaction to his book, the *Noli Me Tangere*. He arrived in Manila on August 5, 1887 and stayed in Calamba until February 1888. As expected, he experienced various forms of harassment from the friars and the Spanish authorities during his sojourn. Concerned with the danger he was facing, his family and friends convinced Rizal to leave the Philippines once again.

Second Travel Abroad

Rizal travelled again to Europe, staying there for four years and five months (1888 to 1892). This time, he took the eastward route to Europe, leaving Manila on February 3, 1888, passing by Hongkong, Japan, and the United States, and returning via Asia. He circumnavigated the world!

He stayed in Hongkong for about 15 days, when he studied Chinese customs and theater and visited the Portuguese colony of Macau. He then left for Japan and stayed there for 45 days, at the Spanish Legation in Yokohama, and visited Tokyo, Nikko, Hakone, etc. He left Japan despite the post offered him by the Spanish charge d'affaires.

He arrived in San Francisco on April 28, 1888 and then took an intercontinental journey by train through the United States, passing by Oakland, Sacramento, Salt Lake, Provo, Ogden, Reno, Colorado, Omaha, Chicago, Niagara, Albany and arriving in New York on May 13, 1888. He left New York on May 16 for Liverpool, and finally to London.

Rizal stayed in London to conduct research at the British Museum and publish an annotation of Morga's *Sucesos de Las Islas Filipinas*. He visited France and hurriedly moved to Brussells, Belgium, given the high cost of living and environment not conducive to writing his new novel, *El Filibusterismo*. At this time, his family's situation in the Philippines turned from bad to worse, his family being evicted from their home. This prompted him to go home. In his letter to Blumentritt, he wrote: *"I have to return to the Philippines. Life is becoming a burden to me here. I have to give an example not to fear death even if this may be terrible...I'm going to meet my destiny...It is better to die than to live miserably."* But he did not have money and wanted to finish writing his novel first. Unhappy with his failed attempt to fight for his family's case in the Spanish Supreme Court, coupled with his disappointment with the Filipinos in Madrid, he decided to abdicate his leadership position in the Filipino community, retired from the *La Solidaridad*, and took a vacation in Biarritz at the French Riviera to finish writing the *El Filibusterismo*. He then went to Ghent, Belgium to print his book through the help of Valentin Ventura.

He sailed from Marseilles on October 18, 1891 and arrived in Hongkong. There, he rented a house, opened a clinic and practiced his profession. While in Hongkong, he made plans for the establishment of a Filipino colony in North Borneo and even visited the place, but this project proved unsuccessful. He also prepared the constitution of *La Liga Filipina* and planned to organize it upon his return to the Philippines.

He returned to Manila on June 20, 1892 against the advice of his family and friends, and immediately went on a trip to Pampanga and Bulacan to meet with Filipino leaders regarding the establishment of *La Liga Filipina*. His organizing activities, however, were short-lived as the Governor General issued a decree on July 12, 1892 banishing him to Dapitan, a secluded place in Mindanao.

Dapitan Interlude

Rizal noted that he was exiled in Dapitan for *"four years, thirteen days and a few hours."* Although it cannot be considered technically as a "travel," Rizal's deportation to Dapitan gave him the opportunity to see other places in the Philippines' South. While in Dapitan, he kept himself busy – practicing medicine, building a school for boys, building a water system for the community, creating a relief map of Mindanao, engaging in beautification activities, doing scientific research on the flora and fauna of the place and contributing to scientific societies in Europe, engaging in business and agriculture, etc.

But Rizal did not feel at ease and was not happy with his situation. As an exile, he felt constrained at doing anything for the good of the country and his fellowmen. He expressed this sentiment to Blumentritt, who advised him to offer his services as a physician to the Spanish forces fighting against the Cuban revolutionaries. He sent in his request to the Spanish governor general who approved it after a long wait.

Rizal left Dapitan on July 31, 1896 via Dumaguete, Cebu and Iloilo. He visited various friends in Dumaguete including Herrero Regidor, then judge in Dumaguete, and also operated on a Spanish captain of the Guardia Civil. In Cebu, he visited a certain Attorney Mateos and performed two operations aside from going to Fort San Pedro. He left Cebu on August 3 for Iloilo where he visited Molo and its famed church, had a brief stopover in Capiz and proceeded to Manila via Romblon. He arrived on August 6, but missed the ship bound for Spain. Nevertheless, he was allowed to stay on board the cruiser Castilla from August 6 to September 2 while waiting for the next outward-bound ship. Meanwhile, the secretive *Katipunan* was discovered by Spanish authorities. The Philippine revolution started.

Third Travel Abroad

With the Spanish government's approval, Rizal embarked again on his third and last travel abroad. On September 3, he left Manila, passing by Singapore where he refused advice of friends to stay behind.

He passed by Ceylon, Suez Canal and reached Barcelona on October 3, when he was promptly arrested and held at the Castle of Montjuich. From there he was brought back to Manila. He arrived a month after and was imprisoned in Fort Santiago while awaiting trial. He was tried, convicted, and executed by musketry on December 30, 1896.

Further Thoughts on Rizal's Travels

Rizal's life was indeed full of comings and goings, of traveling from one place to another. What were his thoughts on travel, and what did he gain from it?

In his essay, *Los Viajes*, Rizal shared his thoughts on travel and the many great things that come with it. In the first place, he saw travel as part of human life and believed that God meant for man to travel. According to him:

> *"The desire to travel as well as to know is so innate in man that it seems that Providence has put it in each one of us, so that, spurred by it, we may study and admire*

His works, communicate and fraternize with those who are far from us, and united, form a single family – the aspiration of all thinkers. For this purpose, He has made man a cosmopolite. He created seas for ships to glide on… the wind to push them… and the stars to guide them even in the darkest night."

He believed that travel enables one to experience things first hand, rather than learning about them through books. He wrote:

"He who knows the surface of the earth and the topography of a country only through the examination of maps…is like a man who learns the opera of Meyerbeer or Rossini by reading only reviews in the newspapers. The brush of landscape artists Lorrain, Ruysdael, or Calame can reproduce on canvas the sun's ray, the coolness of the heavens, the green of the fields, the majesty of the mountains…but what can never be stolen from Nature is that vivid impression that she alone can and knows how to impart – the music of the birds, the movement of the trees, the aroma peculiar to the place – the inexplicable, something the traveler feels that cannot be defined and which seems to awaken in him distant memories of happy days, sorrows and joys gone by, never to return."

His inquisitiveness about what goes on in places he visited almost led to his deportation while he was in Berlin. As Viola (Travels with Rizal) puts it, Rizal was traveling in Europe without a passport when a German police officer asked for his passport and he could not present any. It turned out that Rizal was under surveillance due to his visiting cities, towns, and villages for prolonged periods. The government had interpreted all those steps he had taken as acts of espionage in favor of the government of France. Dr. Rizal admitted that he had been to those places, in Viola's words, *"not for any illicit motive but for purely instructive purpose. Desiring to study the ethnography of a nation, he had adopted the principle of making his preliminary investiga-*

tion in the towns or the smallest villages where the customs and ways of living of the people are simple and natural, unlike in the large cities where those characteristics were more or less modified by artificial culture. " Fortunately, his explanation sufficed.

Although he travelled to and enjoyed the sights and sounds of large cities, Rizal was more enamored with the natural beauty of the places he visited and praised the nature tours they offered. He could be considered a precursor of the movement toward ecotourism. In his impromptu speech to the Tourists' Club of Leitmeritz, he said:

> *"...To the tourists here, nature is the object of admiration and of a very special cult that serves to exalt the soul...For this reason, I admire the activity of the members of the Tourists' Club, because, instead of taking the traveler to the noisy life, to the bars and bright spots of the cities, they invite the man with a heart and soul to acquire new strength for the struggle of life to the bosom of nature, pure, sublime, and enchanting. "*

Travel was an important facet of Rizal's education and sophistication. With it, he learned the culture and politics of other countries, enabling him to understand and compare the Philippines with those countries he visited. This was part of the so-called *"secret mission"* that his elder brother Paciano impressed upon him, for which he was sent overseas – to observe keenly the life and the culture, languages and customs, industries, commerce and government and laws of the European nations in order to prepare himself in the task of liberating his people from Spanish tyranny.

He developed lasting impressions of these foreign countries (Rizal: Reminiscences and Travels) and encountered what he called as *"el demonio de las comparaciones"* (the specter of comparisons) through which he was able to compare and contrast the situation in those countries he visited with that in the Philippines. He found Barcelona at first unfavorable, but later saw it as a great city with an atmosphere of freedom and liberalism, with open-hearted, hospitable and courageous people. He was fascinated with Paris for its architectural wonders, impressed by the freedom the French people enjoyed though openly criticizing the government. He was also enchanted by Geneva, for the ability of its people to speak several languages: French, German and Italian. He described Germany as *"a country with high order and obedience, attractive and praiseworthy morals and women"* and felt *"captivated by its scientific atmosphere and absence of racial discrimination."* Impressed by Germany's efficiency and its scientific milieu, Rizal spent some time in various cities in Germany to study science and become a member of learned societies, as well as to observe its economic and political conditions.

Rizal stayed longer in Japan than intended, *"for the country seems to me very interesting and because in the future we shall have much to do and to deal with Japan."* He wrote:

> *"There are very few thieves among the Japanese. ...houses are left open; their walls are made of paper, and in the hotels one can leave money on the table without fear of losing it. The Japanese are very merry and they are courteous; in the streets, fighting is not seen. Their houses are clean. Rarely are beggars seen. They are very industrious..."*

And he was impressed by the United States – by its material progress as shown in great cities, huge farms, flourishing industries and big factories; the drive and energy of its people; the natural beauty of the land; its high standard of living; and opportunities for a better life. He wrote: *"Undoubtedly America is a great country, but it still has many defects. There is no real civil liberty... However, as they say rightly, America offers a home to the poor who like to work."* His knowledge of the history and politics of these foreign countries enabled him to develop a world view with which he made predictions in his essay "The Philippines a Century Hence."

His travels to Europe also exposed him to the ideas brought by the enlightenment which focused on the advancement of individual liberty, social progress, tolerance, scientific knowledge, constitutional government, and the separation of church and state, among others. His knowledge of Spanish, French, German and English, which he perfected during his travels, enabled him to read the writings of the great philosophers of the time: Descartes, Locke, Spinoza, Rousseau, Voltaire, Hume, Hugo, etc. These ideas helped develop and mold his social and political thinking.

It was while traveling that he found time to write various essays on the Philippine situation as well as his two novels that became the spark-plug of Filipino nationalism and the Philippine revolution against Spain. The *Noli Me Tangere* was written during his first travel abroad: *"One-half...was written in Madrid, one-fourth in Paris, and the rest in Germany."* The sequel, *El Filibusterismo*, was written during his second travel abroad, with parts of it written during his stays in London, Madrid, Paris, Brussels, Biarritz, and Ghent.

It was through travel that he was able to pursue advanced studies in various disciplines which turned him to become the genius that he was. He was able to study medicine and obtain specialization from among the best ophthalmologists in Europe – Spain, France and Germany. In addition to meeting the top scholars and scientists in Europe, he delved into other fields of study and became a member of learned societies such as the Ethnographic Society of Berlin, the Anthropological Society of Berlin, and the Geographic Society of Berlin. It was these contacts that prompted him to establish the short-lived International Association of Filipinologists and to propose an international conference on the Philippines during the Paris World Exposition in 1889.

It was through his travels that he found love, albeit fleeting. Rizal met all the loves of his life outside his hometown of Calamba. Leonor Rivera (age 15) was from Camiling, Tarlac; Leonor Valenzuela (age 14) was from Pagsanjan, Laguna; and Segunda Katigbak (age 14) was from Lipa, Batangas. The other women who were amorously associated with him were foreigners whom he met during his sojourn in foreign countries and during his exile. Consuelo Ortiga y Reyes (age 18) was a Spaniard whom he met in Madrid; O Sei San (age 22), was the daughter of a Japanese samurai whom he met in Tokyo; Gertrude Beckett (age 19) was an English woman from London; Suzanne Thill (age 18) was a Belgian whom he met in Ghent; Nellie Boustead (age 19), an Anglo-French lady, was from Biarritz, France; and Josephine Bracken (age 18), was an Irish lady whom he met in Dapitan.

The Unhappy Camper

But while he had positive thoughts about his travels, which were very productive and gave him much opportunities for self-development, Rizal saw himself as a sad and unhappy pilgrim.

Rizal expressed his unhappiness in his poem, "Song of the Traveler" (*Canto del Viajero*), written just before he embarked on his third travel abroad. In this melancholic poem, he showed the loneliness and the void that he felt as a traveler, likening himself (the traveler) to a withered and fallen leaf tossed about by the wind – ever driven by an invisible power to roam the world, *"without purpose, without love, without country or soul."*

Why "without purpose"? It was probably that his travels were not his own making; they were rather brought on him by circumstances. His early stay in Manila for his studies was cut short because of racial discrimination at the University of Santo Tomas, and his first travel to Europe was arranged by his brother and uncle, without his parents and himself being privy to it. His second trip to Europe was also forced on him by circumstances; it was for his security – to escape from the persecutions by Spanish authorities because of the publication of the *Noli Me Tangere*. His deportation to Dapitan was again not of his own choosing, while his third travel to Europe was prompted by his unhappiness as an exile and probably because of the gathering clouds of revolution that he did not want to be a part of. Through all these, however, he was a pilgrim vainly and hopelessly searching for something – which he referred to as *"treacherous fortune, fortune which e'en as he grasps at it flees."* This goal, this evasive "fortune," this impossible dream, undoubtedly refers to the emancipation of the Philippines from the shackles of Spanish rule.

While working for that goal, he was unhappy with what he found in Spain, particularly the lack of morals and nationalism on the part of the Filipino expatriates there, who were more interested in talking about the buttons of their suits than the situation at home. He, too, was unhappy with the politics in the Filipino community and the lack of unity. In his letter to Paciano, he said: *"What I regret most is that many of our countrymen, poisoned by this environment...seek fame at the cost of money and self-respect, not on their own merits but with banquets and exhibitionism; they do not know that such fame is like a burning scrap of paper, leaving only ashes that afterwards stain and spoil."* He was likewise unhappy with the agrarian trouble that beset his family and the people of Calamba, and his failure to settle them with the Spanish authorities in Manila and Madrid. He felt guilty for being the cause of his family's sufferings. He wrote Blumentritt: *"What has become of my family? When I think of them, I am overcome by such sorrow that, if I had less faith in God, I would have done something foolish...when I think that everyone, my parents, brothers, friends, nephews and nieces, have to suffer in my name, then I feel immensely unfortunate and lose all feelings of gladness."*

He was also not happy with the ineffectiveness, and eventual demise, of the propaganda movement. He himself declared that it was useless to continue the struggle in Madrid, outside the Philippines, eventually concluding that for it to succeed, it had to be done in the Philippines. In his letter to Blumentritt on December 30, 1891, he said: *"That is why I think that La Solidaridad is no longer the place to give battle; this is a new fight. I should like to follow your wishes, but I believe that it will be all in vain; the fight is no longer in Madrid. It is all a waste of time."* Even his attempt at establishing a Filipino agricultural colony in North Borneo failed. And in spite of the various projects he did in Dapitan, he remained unhappy with his situation. In his letter to his sister Trinidad he said: *"I am beginning to feel unwell. I do not think I can endure much longer the kind of life I lead here: much work, poor food, and not a few troubles."*

He mentioned in his poem the void that *"saddens his soul by the absence of love."* Why "without love"? He was referring here to the loneliness he suffered on account of his separation from his loved ones, particularly his family. As somebody who had spent a big part of his life abroad, Rizal missed the companionship and affection of his family and friends. One can easily see this in the exchange of letters between Rizal and his family while he was abroad. He expressed his homesickness by urging his sisters to write more often as he misses them. In his letters from Dapitan, he told his family that the things he missed the most were his family and freedom.

His unhappiness extended to his love life, too. The loss of Leonor Rivera, the sadness over leaving O Sei San, the barrier that prevented him from marrying Nellie Boustead, and the brief amorous flings he had had, created heartbreaks on his part. While he eventually found love in Josephine Bracken, he was generally regretful of his love life, seeing himself *"like those travelers who go through a path strewn with flowers. They pass by without touching them with the hope of finding something uncertain, and the road becomes more arid and they find themselves at last in a bare region, regretting the past."* (Rizal: Reminiscences and Travels). He was already 33 years old when he finally decided to get married, but even this one was taken away from him as the Church disallowed it. Although he settled down with Josephine Bracken as his common law wife, a further source of heartache came when Josephine gave birth to a still-born child and, later on, when he had to leave her to go to Cuba. He knew Josephine was not happy too, addressing her as *"my unhappy wife."*

He expressed doubts as to what future his travels would bring. His despair led him to think that his wanderings may eventually lead to his death abroad *("chance may assign him a tomb on the desert")*, or that he may be able to return home in the future only to find nothing except the *"ashes of love and the tomb of his friends."*

But while the poem expresses his pent-up feelings for the grief he suffered as a traveler, he concluded that it was pointless to complain about his sufferings, for *"dry are the tears that a while for thee ran."* He concluded that he should rather forget about his afflictions, for the world really doesn't care - *"loud laughs the world at the sorrows of man."*

Indeed, Rizal, the traveler, saw himself as a stranger in the land of his birth. As a Filipino who was acculturated abroad, he felt he could never be truly accepted abroad as anything more than an outsider to his native country, unfit to live in it. Thus, he ended up being a native and a foreigner, a stranger *"soon by the world and his country forgotten."*

It is of interest to note that Rizal spent much of his travel time abroad, not locally. His travels in the Philippines were limited – in Luzon, the farthest north was Dagupan, and the farthest south was Laguna. He had never been to Ilocos, the Cordillera, or the Bicol region in Luzon. In addition, had he not been exiled to Dapitan, he would not have been able to see certain parts of the Visayas and Mindanao. But then, his travels and stays abroad were sort of "forced" on him by circumstances. Besides, his was a short life, and the question remains: had he lived longer, could he have travelled more within his own country?

Final Thoughts

In closing, travel was an integral part of Rizal's life, from his childhood to his death. It was, according to him, "… *the dream of the young when they became conscious of the life around them; it is a book for mature men, at the age when the mind is eager to learn; and in fine, it is the last farewell of the old man when he takes his leave of the world to undertake the most mysterious of all voyages.*" To him, "*travel is a caprice in childhood, a passion in youth, a necessity in manhood, and an elegy in old age*" (Rizal, On Travel).

Rizal's travels shaped the person that he came to be. No doubt it brought him sufferings. Had he not travelled, however, he likely would not have had gotten the knowledge and education he gained, the experiences he encountered, the ideas that shaped his thoughts, the literary and political works he produced, the friendships he formed, the loves he met, and the status and honor of an internationally-renowned hero that he was. Travel was a source of his unhappiness, but it was also the source of his triumphs.

References

Diosdado G. Capino, Maria Minerva A. Gonzales, Filipinas E. Pineda, *Rizal's Life, Works and Writings – Their Impact on Our National Identity*, 1977, Google Books.

Austin Craig, *Lineage, Life and Labors of Jose Rizal*, Project Guttenberg eBook, 2005.

Jose Rizal, *Reminiscences and Travels*, National Historical Commission of the Philippines, Manila, 2011.

Jose Rizal, *Political and Historical Writings*, National Historical Commission of the Philippines, Manila, 2011.

Jose Rizal, *Correspondence with Fellow Reformers*, National Historical Commission of the Philippines, Manila, 2011.

Jose Rizal, *Letters with Family Members*, National Heroes Commission, Manila, 2011.

Jose Rizal, *My Last Farewell*, translation by Charles Derbyshire, in https://www.univie.ac.at/ksa/apsis/aufi/rizal/rzpoem2.htm

Jose Rizal, *Song of the Traveler*, translation by Arthur P. Fergusson, in https://www.univie.ac.at/ksa/apsis/aufi/rizal/rzpoem3.htm

Laong Laan, "On Travel," in *Rizal's Prose*, Jose Rizal National Centennial Commission, Manila, 1962.

Leon Ma. Guerrero, *The First Filipino*, National Historical Institute, Manila, 2008.

Maximo Viola, "Travels with Rizal," in Jose Rizal, *Reminiscences and Travels*, National Historical Commission of the Philippines, Manila, 2011.

Appendices

Song of the Traveler by Jose Rizal
translated by Arthur P. Ferguson

Like to a leaf that is fallen and withered,
Tossed by the tempest from pole unto pole;
thus roams the pilgrim abroad without purpose,
Roams without love, without country or soul.

Following anxiously treacherous fortune,
Fortune which e 'en as he grasps as it flees;
Vain though the hopes that his yearning is seeking,
Yet does the pilgrim embark on the seas!

Ever impelled by the invisible power,
Destined to roam from the East to the West;
Oft he remembers the faces of loved ones,
Dreams of the day when he, too, was at rest.

Chance may assign him a tomb on the desert,
Grant him a final asylum of peace ;
Soon by the world and his country forgotten,
God rest his soul when his wanderings cease!

Often the sorrowing pilgrim is envied,
Circling the globe like a sea-gull above;
Little, ah, little they know what a void
Saddens his soul by the absence of love.

Home may the pilgrim return in the future,
Back to his loved ones his footsteps he bends;
Naught will he find but the snow and the ruins,
Ashes of love and the tomb of his friends.

Pilgrim, begone! Nor return more hereafter,
Stranger thou art in the land of thy birth;
Others may sing of their love while rejoicing,
Thou once again must roam o'er the earth.

Pilgrim, begone! Nor return more hereafter,
Dry are the tears that a while for thee ran;
Pilgrim, begone! And forget thine affliction,
Loud laughs the world at the sorrows of man.

This is a revised version of a talk delivered during the Rizal Day celebration sponsored by the Knights of Rizal-Hawaii Chapter on December 30, 2018 at the United Visayan Community Hall in Waipahu, Hawaii.

RIZAL IN THE DIGITAL AGE[*]

Sir Elihu A. Ybañez, KGCR

I HOPE EVERYBODY is having a wonderful time. I want to start by thanking some of our outstanding leaders who are here: Trustees of the Supreme Council, Sir Mel Garraton (USA Central Regional Commander), Sir Randy Datu (Texas Area Commander), Sir Pete Ellorin (Texas Deputy Area Commander), Sir Archie Zalun (Makabayan Chapter Commander), Sir Ben Ongoco (Founder of Houston Chapter), Lady Belle Datu (Founder of Kababaihang Rizalista, Inc.), and Lady Ludy Ellorin (President of Kababaihang Rizalista, Inc.). We are honored to be joined by our fellow knights, ladies, and distinguished guests.

One of the greatest privileges of being a knight is serving as Supreme Commander to outstanding men imbued with Rizal's patriotic zeal and ideals. My optimism about the Order moving forward to new stages of opportunities and strength is because of all of you and our affiliates. I thank you, brother knights and ladies, for your service and commitment.

It is a pleasure to join you as you celebrate this occasion of leadership transition and of recognizing paragons of excellence in the fields of medicine, engineering, nursing, medical technology, education, and community service. I would like to congratulate the incoming officers of the Order – Central USA, Texas Area, Pilar Campos – as well as the new officers and members of *Kababaihang Rizalista*, Inc. Affairs like this bespeak the importance of leadership. It is my hope that you profit from Rizal's wealth of wisdom, teachings, and vision as you serve and fulfill your obligations. May his example provide strategic guidance in all your dealings and decisions. I wish you great success! Likewise, allow me to congratulate our laureates – those who will receive the Dr. Jose P. Rizal Excellence Award. We are grateful that we can acknowledge the work that you do. This is the right time to start thinking of how the award may be used for the advancement of your particular area of interest and how your excellence can reach its maturity by serving the greater good.

We are living through one of the best periods of the Order's life. According to recent figures, global active internet users now total 3.175 billion. What's more, mobile users constitute half of the world population, with two million smart phones being sold worldwide everyday.[1] It is no secret that the technological advancements of digital age have had a progressive impact on knowledge sharing, transmission of information, and reducing barriers of communication.[2]

This means that we have the opportunity to increase the impact and visibility of the Order by tapping the power of social media and integrating technology into our organizational strategy. We cannot afford to show reluctance in implementing breakthrough technologies and choose to cling to old methods. It is said that while many aspects of leadership remain the same, there is a new requirement. We now need DQ or digital quotient - it is no longer just IQ and EQ.[3] As leaders, we should leverage digitization[4] because technological advancement has created a ripple effect that is changing the values and habits of our youth. It is, thus, necessary for us to move with the times so that we can remain relevant and we can properly equip our tech-savvy youth to awaken their ideas of excellence and sense of patriotism.

We have talked a lot about the need to look harder at our chapters, being honest with ourselves about the obstacles to membership, and being open to change so that we can make the Order not only the attractive choice but a viable choice. But I think we haven't been talking enough about branding. Today, an average person is bombarded with philanthropic messages and calls-to-action throughout every avenue. With so many organizations shouting on their bullhorns that their causes are the most important, what makes the Order stand out? How do we ensure that our message is truly heard?

The extent to which people pay attention to what we have to say depends on the strength of our brand. And we can measure the strength of our brand by our reputation and our visibility. In the past, branding was seen as belonging only to the business world. In our modern times, that is no longer the case and mission-driven organizations can stand to benefit from jumping into the branding scene.[5] In order to build a successful and authentic brand, we have to start with the values that form our organizational culture. To successfully communicate the Order's brand to different audiences, we need to know what we want to say, what people can expect from our organization, and the good that we are offering to society. We need a tagline or positioning statement that sets us apart from the rest of the organizations.

Moreover, relatability is important. We must send the message that anyone can advance our mission. We should definitely recognize big fundraisers, but it's also important to show how anyone else can make an impact on our cause by using our website, blogs, and social media accounts to highlight individuals supporting our undertakings.[6] Positioning the Order as a forward-thinking and innovative organization can also be an effective brand strategy. Adopting new technologies and strategies can attract people who may not have been interested in our cause before.[7] Whether we've been consciously cultivating it or not, our organization has a brand. The associations and ideas people have about the Order affect our engagement and social impact.[8]

We know that Dr. Jose P. Rizal was a futurist. He was very much a person ahead of his time. Rizal would have been the type of person that the young people could really emulate, could be inspired by, and somebody who could grab their attention. And I think that he would have loved the Internet.[9] In millennial parlance, Rizal would have been an "influencer".

In conclusion, it is hoped that you will do your part in expanding the reach of our Order using tools in the digital age so that we can effectively propagate Rizal's principles and philosophies. Let us brace ourselves and strengthen our hands for the good work ahead.

Thank you!

End Notes

[1]Brockbank, James. "How technology is changing the way we see the world". citybaseapartments.com. https://www.citybaseapartments.com/blog/how-technology-is-changing-the-way-we-see-the-world/ [Date Accessed: August 20, 2018].

[2] "How non-profits can prepare for the digital age". 42strategies.com. http://42strategies.com/nonprofits-can-prepare-digital-age/ [Date Accessed: August 20, 2018].

[3] Ranade, Prashant. "Leadership in the Digital Age". ceo.com. https://www.ceo.com/operations/leadership-in-the-digital-age/ [Date Accessed: January 22, 2018].

[4] Bouee, Charles-Edouard. "Leadership in the digital age". rolandberger .com. https://www.rolandberger.com/en/Blog/Leadership-in-the-digital-age ..html [Date Accessed: January 23, 2018].

[5] Lumbres, Jastine. "Why Nonprofit Branding Is Important". elevate-click.som https://www.elevateclicks.com/the-nonprofit-marketing-blog/why-nonprofit-branding-is-important [Date Accessed: August 20, 2018].

[6] Gauss, Allison. "5 Smart Brand Strategies for Nonprofits". classy.org. https://www.classy.org/blog/5-smart-brand-strategies-nonprofits/ [Date Accessed: August 20, 2018].

[7] *Ibid.*

[8] *Ibid.*

[9] Excerpt from the statement of My Rizal 150 organizer Maite Gallego. https://sg.news.yahoo.com/blogs/the-inbox/rediscovering-rizal-putting-fili-filipino-064847862.html [Date Accessed: August 21, 2018].

Without education and liberty, which are the soil and sun of man, no reform is possible, no measure can yield the result desired.

Jose P. Rizal

Part II
RIZAL IN EDUCATION

Rizal and Education

Patricia Espiritu-Halagao, PhD

OOD EVENING. Thank you for the introduction. Distinguished guests, I am honored to be among so many people in the Filipino community that I look up to and admire. The Knights of Rizal's ideals of "Freedom, equality, respect for human worth and dignity, love for country, appreciation of heritage and democratic principles" represent many of my beliefs and values.

First and foremost, I would like to dedicate my speech to my first doctoral student, Dr. Julius Soria, who recently passed away from cancer. Julius' family and friends held a service for him this morning. Through his work in heritage language and Ilokano, Julius truly embodied the spirit and values of Jose Rizal. Dr. Soria was a gifted educator and I know that his work will live on through the lives of the many students he touched during his short time on this earth.

I would like to take this opportunity to thank Manong Jun Colmenares and your organization for asking me to speak at your special night. Over the years, I have come to know Manong Jun and have a great deal of respect for him. I admire his quiet and persistent ways of how he makes things happen in his professional work, commitment to organizations, and special projects like Florentino Das story.

As I have learned more about the Knights of Rizal, I am impressed with your organization and would like to extend my congratulations to this year's recipient of promoting peace and social justice in the community and across society. I am also excited to learn about your Rizalian Youth Council and the new Rizalian Women's Council.

When asked to present at your gala, I jumped at the

opportunity to learn more about our Philippine hero, Dr. Jose Rizal. I was eager to delve more into his life and connect to his philosophies and theories of education.

So being the academic I am, I begin with research. Manong Jun recommended the book *Rizal and Education* by Camilo Osias published in 1921. Mr. Osias gleaned insights into Dr. Rizal's attitudes toward education and youth by examining his actions, writings and the characters in his books. As I was reading *Rizal and Education*, I started to see how Rizal's philosophies and practices were ahead of his time, and relevant to today's approaches to education. It made me even think and ask the question: How do I live Jose Rizal in my life as an educator?

I want to share three areas where I see Dr. Rizal's work come out in my life – the focus of my research, my practices as a teacher, and my policies as a former member of the Hawaii State BOE, all of which feeds into my overarching service to our Filipino community.

One aspect that struck out first in my reading is Jose Rizal's centering on youth and dependence on them for our future. In an address he gave in Europe, he stated that the youth are the "the sacred hope of the fatherland." He found education to be the most important step to freeing our people -- a pre-requisite to the liberation of his people.

The first step in liberation is consciousness. It is bringing to light and being aware of the issue or problem. Knowledge is gained through education.

Research
My research brings attention to the educational experiences of Filipino Americans in our state and nation. Let's start first with numbers. I am sure you are aware that Filipinos make up the largest ethnic group in Hawaii, with Filipinos and part Filipinos representing close to 25%.

How about in our schools? What do you think is the largest

ethnic group in our schools? When I ask this to teachers, most often they say "Japanese." However, Native Hawaiians make up 24%, with Filipinos closely behind at 22%. Together Hawaiians and Filipinos make up close to the majority of our schools. Despite our historical presence and high numbers in our schools, there is little attention paid towards Filipinos as an ethnic group. Further, research on Filipinos in education is woefully lacking.

I have made it my mission to expose the achievement gaps, opportunities, and needs of our student population. In October, the first special edition on Filipinos in education in the journal *Educational Perspectives* will be published. I contributed an article that examines the student achievement and opportunities of Filipinos in our public school system from all different angles.

Despite the fact that Filipinos make up 22% of our K-12 students in Hawaii public schools, we only make up 9% at UH Manoa, our university system's flagship campus.

Among educators, Filipinos only make up 6% of our public school teachers and only 2% of our UH faculty.

While we've made progress in some areas, the journal brings out these challenges and discrepancies to light and discusses issues of language, legacy of colonization, but more importantly solutions emerging from our own scholars on how we can move the needle to disrupt these persistent gaps over time. We need to make sure education liberates us and does not reify the structures of power that keep our people down.

In my article, I talk about the impact of culturally relevant education on academic achievement. Research shows that when learning is situated within the lived experiences of students, it is more meaningful, have higher interest appeal, and are learned more easily. As a result, the academic achievement will improve when they are taught through their own cultural and experiential filters.

When I was growing up I did not learn about my culture or the contributions of Filipinos to America in school. So, when I became a teacher, it was important for me to have my students' backgrounds represented and connected to what they learned in school. I went back to graduate school to study multicultural education only to find culture meant African American and Latinos and if there was Asian it was largely Japanese and Chinese Americans. Where were the Filipinos?

I set out to co-develop a multicultural curriculum that looked at history through the lens of Filipinos called *Pinoy Teach*. This wasn't an ordinary curriculum. The idea was to empower college students who learned their Filipino history and culture then team-teach Filipino history and culture to middle school students. Our slogan was: "Knowledge is power, teaching is empowerment." This set up not only allowed classroom teachers to sit back and learn from college students, but Filipino college students became role models to students and many of them went on to become teachers themselves.

Teaching
Let me give you an example of how Pinoy Teach was multicultural and culturally relevant. In every lesson, we had a key concept that we would look at from different perspectives. In one lesson, we taught students about the concept of Revolution. We talked about how any revolution has the three stages—consciousness, propaganda, and armed struggle and how a person could represent each stage. For example, take the American Revolution. Benjamin Franklin represented consciousness because he brought the issues of America to a national stage in France, Thomas Paine represented propaganda through his writing Common Sense, and General George Washington represented armed struggle. Now let's take the same concept and look at the Civil Rights Movement: MLKJ represented consciousness, Black civil rights organizations like NAACP for propaganda, and Malcom X Black Panthers for armed struggle. What would revolution look

like from a Filipino perspective? When looking at Philippine Revolution, Jose Rizal represented consciousness as he sought "to awaken his countrymen to the ills of the country and to the necessity of correcting them," Andres Bonafacio for propaganda through his work with the *Katipunan*, and General Emilio Aguinaldo represented armed struggle. Teaching history through these multiple perspectives teaches universal concepts, similarities and differences across groups. And this positioned a Filipino example that is Rizal to the likes of Benjamin Franklin and Dr. Martin Luther King, a status most deserving.

When I think of the importance of teaching a multicultural history representative of your students, I think of Maria who was a Filipina middle school student that I interviewed who went to a largely Filipino school. I asked her why she had never learned about her history in school. She thought for a minute and answered: "It's probably because Filipinos haven't done anything important." Her answer was like a dagger to my heart, but more importantly revealed, when you don't see yourself in what you read, you are invisible and unimportant.

Pinoy Teach later formed the basis of a curriculum I co-wrote for the Smithsonian Asian Pacific American Center. Launched in 2006 to celebrate the Centennial of First Filipinos to America, we called it iJeepney.com. This curriculum is published online making it available to any teacher in the country to teach about Filipino.

In 2010, I collaborated with UH Faculty who were specialists in Philippine history and languages and Filipino American Studies to develop the Sistan Alhambra Filipino American Education Institute.

This program was named after Sistan Alhambra -- the first Filipina teacher in Hawaii, developed for teachers in Hawaii to know and understand how to better teach our Filipino children in Hawaii.

I see how Jose Rizal's attitudes toward *how* one should teach is aligned to what today we call strength-based education or assets-based education – an antithesis to standards-based education. He flips the model around: instead of beginning with a set of standards, you want students to achieve. You start with what they are good at, building confidence in who they are and engaging them in learning. When Rizal was exiled in Dapitan, he taught a small group of students. He stated: "If one is careless about his lesson, I charged it to lack of desire and never to lack of capacity. I made them think that they were more capable than they really were, which urged them on to study, just as any confidence leads to notable achievements."

I take this same mindset into the policy work I did when I served on the Hawaii State BOE for three years. The BOE sets policy and direction for the entire state. I started out with three main goals: to be an advocate for teachers, marginalized communities like our immigrant, Filipino, Native Hawaiians and Pacific Islanders, and bridge relationship between higher education and K-12.

During my tenure, I was a strong advocate for Hawaiian education policies and well-rounded curriculum. But, I discovered there was no policy for our students classified as English Learners, making us one of only two states in the nation to not have a policy. This troubled me because we did not have a vision of what we wanted for this population who makes up 10% of our population, many whom are Filipinos. I came to learn that Filipino languages make up the majority of the languages that our EL students speak, with Micronesian coming next.

I set out to develop a policy in collaboration with others. I listened to our multilingual community and heard over and over again they wanted their children's culture and languages viewed as assets not as deficits. Many shared stories of their children expressing shame in speaking Tagalog or Ilokano. When we label our students EL, they are viewed as deficit, not knowing English. Instead, we need to change the conversation and call our students multilingual who bring assets to the table.

Who better to look for inspiration and as role model with languages than Jose Rizal. Dr. Rizal lived in Europe for 10 years. During that time, he picked up a number of languages; in fact, he could converse in more than 10 different tongues such as Latin, Hebrew, Arabic, and Greek, French, German, and English, Chinese and Japanese. Of course, he knew Tagalog and Spanish.

In our global world, knowing another language is an asset. We've missed a valuable opportunity to foster our students' strengths to be bilingual in English and Filipino. Studies show that knowing additional language has cognitive benefits. Long standing research shows bilingual education programs are far more effective in learning the content and learning English.

Armed with this knowledge and research, and after two years of engaged policy-making, the BOE adopted two policies: the Seal of Biliteracy and Multilingualism for Equitable Education. Together, these policies encourage students to maintain and keep their home languages and start to put structures in place for more heritage language programs, bilingual education programs (besides Hawaiian immersion) that represent our immigrant languages like Tagalog and Ilokano. In addition, the policies call for more effective teachers, and resources for families.

As a result of being on the BOE, I am at the table bringing to light issues relevant to our community. While I am no longer on the BOE, we are fortunate to have Rizalian Youth Council President Andrea Lyn Mateo at the table. She is in a unique position to advocate for students and Filipinos.

In Service of others
When I read Jose Rizal's work he reminds me of Brazilian philosopher and educator, Paolo Freire, who wrote *Pedagogy of the Oppressed* and saw how education can

liberate people. Like Freire who worked with the poor and helped them to analyze their situations to help them move forward, Osias stated: "our national hero believed in the enlightenment of all classes, farmers and laborers as well as those belonging to the professional classes. I don't see any evil in enlightening those same farmers and laborers in giving them at least an education that will aid them in perfecting themselves and in perfecting their work, in placing them in a condition to understand many things of which they are at present ignorant."

So, what would Jose Rizal say is the purpose of education? Nowadays, the focus is on college and career readiness. Of course, we cannot deny the reality and practicality of an education. However, I do turn to Rizal about the grander purpose of education. When he was talking to a student who wanted to study medicine, he asked whether one is truly accomplished if he "confines [himself] to learning how to put on plasters and apply leeches, and don't ever try to improve or impair the condition of [his] kind."

In one of his famous books, *El Filibusterismo,* Rizal writes about a character, Isagani, and how he represents to him the ideal youth and student who is filled with a spirit of service. Rizal was hopeful that you the Filipino youth shall lead lives of useful service.

Author Osias asks, "We have known Rizal as the greatest Filipino writer, patriot, and reformer. May we not from this day revere him also as the greatest Filipino educator?" I agree. We can learn many lessons from Jose Rizal about education on how we must capitalize on our students' strengths in education; how we must instill knowledge in our children about their history, language and culture; how education should promote pride in one's ethnic identity; how the purpose of education is for service.

Rizal was a highly educated man, well-rounded in his pursuits in life. He used his education not for self-gain or wealth, but he used education to form a strong foundation of his identity, to think critically about his country, and then to take action to improve the lot of his people.

Jose Rizal literally laid down his life for rightness and justice. I ask you: what will we do as a community to create and require an education that is right and just for our Filipino students -- and that would make Dr. Jose Rizal proud?

Studying and Teaching Rizal Under the Shadow of the Marcos Dictatorship

Patricio N. Abinales, PhD

A SEMESTER AFTER I graduated with a B.A. in History at the University of the Philippines, my then boss, the Chair of the Filipino Department and essayist Petronilo Bn. Daroy, asked me if I was interested in teaching two classes of Philippine Institutions 100, the course more known by its description "The Life and Writings of Jose Rizal." The Department needed warm bodies to teach this course that Congress has mandated as a required course that every undergraduate must take to complete his/her college education. With no other "bites" in the job market (what can a History major offer?) I accepted Pete's invitation and so in June 1979, I got promoted from student assistant to lecturer, to be paid P17.00 an hour plus P55.00 per final exam.

I was ready to teach the course having been inspired by my PI 100 professor, Nicanor ("Nick") Tiongson. But I did not start that way: like most young Filipinos I was looking forward to just slogging through the course. The way our high school teachers "taught" Rizal (a minor section in our Civics class) was by telling us to "go buy the comics" at the bookstore, and when we had our quiz, the questions bordered on the trivial: When was he born? Who were Rizal's parents? What were the titles of his two novels? Who were his girlfriends? When and where did he die? The only "serious moment" was when we were assigned to memorize *Mi Ultimo Adios* (the English translation of course!) or *To the Filipino Youth* and recite these in class.

But otherwise, these were the only things we learned about the national hero in high school so that when we enrolled in PI 100, we were looking forward to a humdrum summer.

And we were pleasantly surprised. Nick breathed life into Rizal – giving context to his childhood and his student days, especially when Rizal began to start questioning Spanish racism and organizing his fellow creoles in the same way that we were organizing ourselves as part of a growing anti-dictatorship student movement. The high point in his class was making us read *Noli Me Tangere* and *El Filibuster-ismo*. A back-to-back reading of *Noli* made us hate the friars, commiserate with Ibarra and Maria Clara, be hurt and angered by what Padre Salvi did to Sisa and her kids, idolize Elias, and laugh at the antics of Doña Victorina and Doña Consolacion, with their vain comical attempts to look mestizo and sound Spanish as well as the women sodality group who prayed the whole day to earn more graces from God.

Nick explained to us colonial repression, local elite opportunism and the bravery of Elias in a manner that enabled us to compare our lives under the Marcos dictatorship. Oppression stared us in the face daily. Marcos sent many of our friends to jail, tortured many, while his soldiers killed a couple. Inside campus, the spies kept watch, even "enrolling" in classes of suspected subversive professors who were most likely to attract radicals and activists. The opportunism of some of our professors (a couple of historians) were the researchers and ghost-writers of Marcos – explaining their working as paid hacks as the only viable way to keep the nationalist spirit alive. Then there was Elias – humble and smart, with a rich pedigree that he willingly abandoned to serve the powerless, and a noble character who gave his life so that the naïve Ibarra could go on.

For young activists such as myself then, truly learning about Rizal and his writings for the first time ever put our politics in its firm historical grounding – we were fighting the Marcos dictatorship as part of a longer historical process, a tradition we could claim as having dated back to Rizal and his generation. We felt proud to be legatees of his politics.

But we were also "disappointed" with his reformism. Nick may have finally taught us the "real" Rizal, but as activists, we could not shed off our biases against him, the foremost of which that his political value was limited because he was a reformist. It was a view popularized by the nationalist historian Renato Constantino who claimed that Rizal never indeed repudiated Spanish colonialism. In fact, Constantino argued, Rizal turned his back on Andres Bonifacio and the Katipunan twice – first when the latter's representatives visited him in Dapitan to ask his support for the organization, and second, when word of the Katipunan's uprising in Pugadlawin reached him, he readily boarded a ship bound for Spain and there offer his services as a doctor of the Spanish army in Cuba. After his arrest, Rizal would allegedly go into a tailspin: facing death after a kangaroo court declared him guilty, Rizal retracted his criticism of the Catholic Church.

Constantino would double down in his criticism of Rizal by arguing that it was not Filipinos who made him the national hero. It was the Americans. After having discovered how much Filipinos admired Rizal, a cabal of colonialists led by Governor-General Howard Taft, skillfully stage-managed the political resurrection of Rizal. They argued that Rizal was the better of all his peers when it came to the question of national independence. He favored gradualism over radicalism, education over revolution, and tutelage training (a phrase the Americans loved to invoke) over hastily-formed Republics. It also helped that Filipinos at that time were still fiercely anti-Spanish and anti-friar. In promoting Rizal, the Americans could say they were on his side against the prayles and the Kastilaloys; they were also comrades-in-arms when supporting and defending "Reason" and the Enlightenment.

These were powerful arguments by an armchair revolution that appealed to among my peers who saw national salvation in the Communist Party of the Philippines' "national democratic revolution" via protracted armed struggle. Rizal was indeed the "opportunist," the more extremist of them argued, and he did not deserve the honor of being the nation's hero. It should have been Andres Bonifacio!

We completed Nick's class with a better, even more profound, understanding of Rizal, but we also emerged out of that summer session convinced that Constantino was right. Rizal did not deserve his place as the country's "First Filipino." I brought all these beliefs with me as I headed to my first class at the fourth floor of UP's historic "Arts and Sciences (AS)" building to a group of junior and senior students, some only a year younger than I was, three even my dormitory-mates at the other famous UP icon, Narra Residence Hall. And I began duplicating Nick's class, his fantastic analyses of Rizal, but also along with my activist bias against the National Hero.

I would teach PI 100 for the next 9 years. It was a tremendous complimentary income to my regular salary as a research assistant at UP's Third World Studies Center. Marcos was still in power, and while I began to distance myself from a movement that glorified the Khmer Rouge and Mao's brutal Great Proletarian Cultural Revolution, I still discussed with my students the issues of the times to animate them to participate in the struggle against the Marcos dictatorship.

But along the way, I would discover new gems about Rizal and his writings. Consider, for example, the Noli and several of its characters. Take the case of Maria Clara. Crisostomo Ibarra's girlfriend is often associated with Inang Pilipinas as, like the country, she was this pristine, warm person who Padre Salvi proceeds to abuse and rape at the end of the novel. A more cynical view of Maria Clara was that she was the anti-woman, a character Rizal created to provide contrast to the women he admired the most – his mother and the women of Malolos, Bulacan, who wrote a letter to the Spanish governor-general demanding that he require Spanish in children's schools. Feminists derided her also for being weak-minded, of unquestioningly following the dictates of the men in her life, from her two fathers (birth Dad Padre Damaso, and adoptive parent, Capitan Tiago), and her boyfriend Ibarra. Why her lines are even so petty and facile, my feminist friends pointed out. She was *mahinhin* and *walang isip.*

But after a couple of years reading and rereading this classic novel, I soon realized that Rizal's Maria Clara was a far more complex character. Yes, Rizal possibly made her the icon of Inang Filipinas, but it was a nation not of "pure-breed" Malays; it was a nation of creoles and mestizos/mestizas who are born out of wedlock. The evidence is right there staring us in the face: Maria Clara's father was a Spanish friar who either forced himself on her mother Pia Alba (the wife of Kapitan Tiago), or became her lover (there is a hint in the novel that Tiago was probably not interested in sex, being so engrossed with his different businesses which included a couple of opium dens). She was not only mestiza (and thus not pure-breed Pinoy!); she was also the love-child of an illicit and immoral relationship.

Neither was Maria Clara always beholden to the men in her life. In fact, in that final scenes of her blissful life, Maria Clara showed more character and courage compared to the men in her life. After his escape from prison, thanks to the help of Elias, a distraught and clearly bewildered Ibarra went to say goodbye to Maria Clara. She immediately sensed the gravity of his confusion and did one thing readers never expected of her – she shed off her timidity and kissed Ibarra! Then after Fr. Salvi convinced Tiago to put Maria Clara back to the nunnery where he was principal confessor and there raped her repeatedly, Maria Clara found refuge in madness where she would be free from all the depravities heaped on her.

When I told my friends about these episodes as evidence of Maria Clara's heroism, they snickered, accusing me of over-reading her character. But if you put these actions within the context of late colonial Spain, where women were – in general – treated as objects of men's love, lusts and fantasy, then what Maria Clara did was exceptional. She did not only show audacity in resisting Salvi and also defying her real father, but she also revealed how bland and sterile Ibarra's views of relationships were, where women were supposed to be these witless damsels in distress to be saved by their men in times of crisis.

No, I think Rizal had more respect towards mestizas and children of wedlock like Maria Clara.

So, too, with Sisa. In the contemporary imagination, she was the working class version of Maria Clara, albeit living a more wretched life than her middle-class counterpart – physically abused by an alcoholic husband, forced to find any kind of work just to get her kids to school, and when accused by the friar of entertaining criminal thoughts, arrested, and made to walk through the center of town in chains and with two members of the *guardia civil* flanking her. I think, for Rizal, she was the better symbol of an oppressed Filipina. She taught her children well. Salvi kicked Crispin to death for failing to time the ringing of the bell, and Basilio escaped and, under the surprising protection of Kapitan Tiago, was able to attend school. I once asked my students where they thought Basilio got his resilience. All of them unanimously answered "Sisa." She went mad in prison, but never did she waver in her sacrifice for her sons.

Now compare these exceptional women to the men. Ibarra was indeed an honorable man and a product of European education. But he was also a clueless buffoon, easily outmaneuvered by Damaso and Salvi, unable to express his love in the open to Maria Clara (the balcony scene where they first met after Ibarra returned is the corniest chapters in the *Noli*), and suspicious of the Elias' entreaties that reforms were urgently needed in the colony and that he should spearhead the movement for change. Ibarra had this patronizing regard towards the rest of San Diego, introducing himself like a German gentleman at Tiago's party. In another chapter, he declares his love for Maria Clara by announcing that he would build her a school! No roses there, I told my students; just a school again to show how much of a European bonhomie he was! All my students sneered).

(I reminded my students that these episodes should tell them of their American-Filipino relatives who visit the old country as *balikbayan* and proceed to show *Pinoy* relatives how much they have done well by speaking only to them in English. One student impishly said, Ibarra sounded more like many UP professors who just returned with their Ph.D. from some school in the European boonies. She added that her American-Filipino relatives actually seemed more like Doña Victorina with their tortured use of American English. We all had a good laugh).

Four years into teaching the course, I found myself more and more immersed in trying to understand Rizal's fascinating mind. The political context had changed. There were reports that the communists New People's Army (NPA) was winning the guerilla war in the countryside and, when the dictatorship had Benigno Aquino, Jr., killed at the airport tarmac, the country erupted in protest. The middle class and even the elites have had enough of Marcos, his chowhound of a wife, his torturers, and cronies. And so did the people.

My students and I became more and more interested in reading Rizal through the prism of the NPA (our present-day Elias!!) and Ibarra, who in *El Filibusterismo*, had returned home, after making money in the Americas, and plotting to plant an improvised explosive device (IED) in the middle of a celebration where all the perfidious elements of colonial society were to congregate. We found ourselves asking more which options would have a lasting positive effect on society – people's war, a nitroglycerine bomb, or the continued pursuit for reforms, which the students in the *Fili* were pushing for until they were ensnared into Simoun's plot. The discussions inevitably returned to Bonifacio and Rizal; who among the historical figures can rally Filipinos apart from the slain Ninoy Aquino?

It must have been the times because my students' exchanges became more and more passionate. There was even one time when they nearly came to blows. (I was able to settle this by calling for a vote instead. Rizal lost). I also found myself canceling classes more often, as there were almost daily protests in the university and outside. This was the time when my activist-students were arguing that one's education would benefit more if they immerse themselves in the so-called "parliament of the streets." I could not agree more, and throughout most of 1984, I would find myself marching with my students along Quezon Avenue down to Plaza Miranda in Quiapo, or around the UP Diliman campus.

Then the dying Marcos announced in December 1985, that he will be holding "snap elections" to determine if Filipinos still wanted him president. Corazon "Cory" Aquino rose up to challenge him. The rest is history.

After the fall of Marcos, I went back to research and teaching PI 100. But this did not last long. In 1988, reeling from the military assassination of two of my best friends a year before (one of them was the student leader Lean Alejandro), and still befuddled by what happened in EDSA in February 1986, I took a leave from UP and went to graduate school.

There, in my new surroundings, I would discover more about Rizal, courtesy of my adviser, the eminent scholar of nationalism, Benedict Anderson. In my first year at Cornell University, Ben was beginning to get interested in the Philippines and was reading as much as he can about home. As expected, he read Rizal's novels. He realized that our national hero's brilliance can best be understood if *Noli Me Tangere* and *El Filibusterismo* were to be read in the original Spanish. Ben started to learn Spanish. What came after that were a series of essays on Rizal that, among other things, added more to the latter's fame, as Ben, this time, introduced him to an international audience.

How this came about and what I learned from this third phase in my encounters with Rizal is another story in itself.

Noli Me Tangere's Ibarra and Elias: How Rizal's Words Create Our Worlds

Eva Rose B. Washburn-Repollo, PhD

WE WERE ALL YOUNG when we left the Philippines. It took courage, for we left the comfort of our homes, no matter how modest, to thrive here in Hawaii. Perhaps we will be a lot braver still, if we can find a way to return home and look back at where we came from using the same stretched and strong roots that have held us till now, to reach our fullest potential.

Such was the life of Jose Rizal. And such was the life of Crisostomo Ibarra, one of the main characters he created in his novel, the *Noli Me Tangere*.

But that was not the life of Elias, the other Jose Rizal.

For those of us who are unfamiliar with *Noli Me Tangere* published in 1887, this is the novel that mirrored the life of the Filipinos and revealed to them their lives in Jose Rizal's words.

Today, the Philippines and the US are under the leadership of men who have forced us to examine our identity, our nationalism and our citizenship. In the USA, we are confronted with identity politics, so polarizing that we see people telling those who dream in this country, that they do not belong here. Instead of acknowledging our identities through our hard work, our intelligence, our love for our children and family, fellow immigrants question and judge each other's right to be here based on their ethnicity.

In Hawaii, we have Filipinos who have proven that they can thrive and succeed in America. We remain vigilant in the struggle to prove to the world just how capable we are.

Whatever space you occupy in this political spectrum, I urge you to consider how this power struggle is embedded in socio-cultural and political discourses.

I teach critical media studies and intercultural communication at Chaminade University. I teach the meaning of culture and how we define ourselves to each other. I also look at words and actions and how we use them to construct ourselves to others. I teach my students cultures like the culture of CLASS, or the cultures of the rich and the poor – two cultures that we hardly look at, convincing ourselves that these are natural arrangements or realities we cannot control. I often tell my students that we learn more when we are uncomfortable. And the hope is to develop in them a worldview that can EMPATHIZE with others who are different. Culture has more than 150 definitions and one of the most telling words in the definition of culture is the word, SURVIVAL. We invent and learn the words that help us survive.

Tonight, I would like to share the worlds in the words of two of *Noli Me Tangere*'s characters, as I believe they embody the worldviews of many Filipinos.

Ibarra and Elias. You and I.

So, today, I will use many of his words, and in our socio-cultural context, I would like to argue that there is in each one of us, an Ibarra and an Elias. I choose these characters because I have met Ibarra and Elias many times in my life. I am a registered Cebuano Visayan court interpreter. My father was a lawyer in the Philippines and he filled our home with stories about his clients, many of them from the world of Elias, trying to survive the courtroom with interpreters who accompanied them into the world of Ibarra.

Our house was like a processing center for conflict, almost like an ER. My father came from humble beginnings. As a child, he remembered times when he walked barefoot from his home, carrying a manila envelope to hold his pencils and papers, writing on banana leaves when he ran out of paper, memorizing words before these faded. Like many lawyers who had poor parents, he fought for people who did not sign their names. In identity politics, your mastery of the foreign tongue is your cultural capital.

I grew up like many of you during a time when speaking English was considered powerful. My mother and father, who were teenagers in the early 50s danced to the music of Elvis Presley, Nat King Cole, Engelbert Humperdinck (who I had the rare chance to see three weeks ago at the Hawaii Theater), Johnny Mathis, Judy Garland and many in that generation. Many of our parents became teachers, earning high status after pursuing advanced degrees from American universities.

Many of the Elias my father defended were identified with a purple thumb print. Often, they were maligned with words like *TAMLA RA KA*, which means that you are nothing but a thumb print. Today, there are still many Filipinos who cannot sign their names.

In Rizal's *Noli Me Tangere*, we first meet Elias when Ibarra and his friends went fishing. He is described as a man with powerful strength. In this chapter, he dives to protect everyone from a vicious crocodile and after looping a rope around its wide mouth the crocodile breaks free. Underwater, Elias was saved by Ibarra when he dove after Elias with a knife that cut the crocodile to its death. To Ibarra, Elias says, "I owe you my life."

Earlier in the novel, Ibarra is described in Elias words: "I have the good fortune of rendering a service to a rich young man of good heart, a noble young man who seeks the welfare of the country. It is said, that he has friends in Madrid; I do not know whether that is true or not, but I can assure you that he is a friend of the Governor General."

Elias, as we know is a stranger in this town. He is described as a fugitive, a vigilante, and a spokesman for the oppressed.

In Chapter 41, entitled "Right and Might," Elias returns the favor to Ibarra. Ibarra asked Elias to break up an impeding riot as the people were approached by the Spanish Constabulary. Ibarra asked Elias how he was able to stop the riot and Elias explained how he has helped many people in such despair that he could command groups to follow his lead. Are people who are like Elias, MIGHTY and are people who are like Ibarra, RIGHT?

In Chapter 46, entitled, "The Oppressed," we see the mighty strength of Elias as he tells Old Man Tasyo how he searched for him on foot, covering two provinces in only 15 days.

Is Elias' native intelligence imprinted on the terrain of his land, a master of the caves and navigator of peaks where mountains meet? Was Elias created after revolutionary heroes before the time of Rizal who were known for their speed likened to the wind and the lightning? DAGOHOY and KILAT. Leon Kilat was from Negros and Francisco Dagohoy, a Boholano, holds the distinction of having initiated the longest revolt in Philippine history, from 1744 to 1828.

So why is it important to take care of the ELIAS in us, to view the world like Elias, and how do we live as IBARRAS?

Jose Rizal's words created these worlds for us.

One night, Elias invites Ibarra to a conversation. He is on a boat with Ibarra, on a peaceful lake. We know the temperament and malleability of water. The significance of balance and peace.

We read Elias and Ibarra as if one is talking to himself, the learned, rich and powerful Ibarra, and the poor, strong, oppressed and determined Elias.

In the story of Elias in Chapter 51, his past and present misfortunes started when his grandfather was accused of burning the store of his master, a Spanish merchant. In this chapter Jose Rizal recounts a furious agony suffered by the servant and his children who were brutally murdered with the sons' limbs cut up and hanged in public view. Elias' father survived as he was still in his grandmother's womb. And later Elias sought to avenge his family's misfortunes. We later find out the Spanish merchant was Ibarra's great grandfather.

Was Rizal Ibarra or Elias, divided and conflicted within his own identity, or was he defining for us the Filipino? Sociocultural and political discourses or the contexts of words are always controlled by those who are in power. Rizal found a way to help us understand the rich and poor. To help us understand, who ... we... can... yet ...be?

Many of us have lived far away, educated like Ibarra. We also know of people back home working under the hot sun, digging *balanghoy, camote* and *gabi,* balancing sacks expertly on top of their heads as they wind their way down rough side roads cemented only by their own constant treks. There are still many of us Filipinos in Hawaii who seek better lives.

So, more about the boat on the lake, Elias is with Ibarra. Equal weight on a boat in a perfectly quiet water. Nothing is stirring except their words. We see ourselves, metaphorically and literally in one boat: how can we define in words the world that we now inhabit if we belong to two different cultures, trying to be Elias, trying to be Ibarra?

On the boat, Ibarra says "I love our country, Elias, as you may love her; I understand somewhat of what is wanted; I have listened attentively to what you have said. Yet, my friend, for all that, I think we have been rather carried away by emotion."

"Forgive me, Sir," answers Elias, shaking his head. "I am

not eloquent enough to convince you. Although I have had a little schooling, I am only a native. You will always doubt my right to say anything and whatever I may say will always be suspect. Those who have given a contrary opinion are Spaniards, and as such, although they may spout trivialities and stupidities, their accent, their titles, and their race make what they say sacred, and give them such authority that I, in spite of my education, may never try again to argue with them."

Ibarra answers, "Elias, your bitter words touch my heart and make me doubt in turn. Well, how can I help it? I was not brought up among the people, and perhaps I do not know what they need. I spent my childhood in the Jesuit school and grew up in Europe. My opinions were formed by books, and I know only what men have brought to light; I know nothing of the things that remain hidden, that have not been written about. For all that, I love our country like you do, not only because it is the duty of every man to love the country that gave them life and which will perhaps be his last refuge, not only because all of my most beautiful memories are alive in it, but also because I owe it and will owe it my happiness."

Elias replies. "And I, because I owe it my misfortunes."

"Let me repeat that," Ibarra says, "I owe it and will owe it my happiness." And Elias replies, "and I, because I owe it my misfortunes."

Do we love our country because it has given us so much? Or, do we love our country because we want to regain what we have lost?

In the *Noli*, we lose Elias.

Will the world of Elias – his strength for hunting, his farm lands and fresh produce, his song and his forests, the caves that protect him, his fresh fish, the waterfalls that caress him, clothes made from abaca fibers – all these, still define who we are? Or, in this country where our unique culture needs to be valued, how can we keep ourselves from being marginalized? We have mastered the foreign tongue and bought into lives of frozen dinners, high heeled shoes – manufactured needs. We have succeeded here. We have seen how our hard work has paid off. Until…we look back, and we try to hear again the songs of our native birds, yearning to reconcile with our new voices.

Will Ibarra exist and continue to flourish without Elias raging mightily deep inside?

Salamat, ug maayong gabii kaninyong tanan!

SA AKING MGA KABATA:
DID THE 8-YEAR OLD RIZAL WRITE THIS TAGALOG POEM?

Sir Floro Quibuyen, Ph.D, KCR

*S*A *AKING MGA KABATA*, supposedly written by Rizal in 1869, is a wonderful poem that has often been cited to promote the Filipino national language. Philippine national artist for literature Nick Joaquin even sees in the poem evidence that the 8-year old Rizal "already saw the coming of Spain as a disastrous storm wrecking the barque of native culture 'in the night of time'." Indeed, notions of a rich indigenous heritage animate the poem:

Kapagka ang baya'y sadyang umiibig
sa kanyang salitang kaloob ng langit,
sanlang kalayaan nasa ring masapit
katulad ng ibong na sa himpapawid.

Pagka't ang salita'y isang kahatulan
sa bayan, sa nayo't mga kaharian,
at ang isang tao'y katulad, kabagay
ng alin mang likha noong kalayaan.

Ang hindi magmahal sa kanyang salita
mahigit sa hayop at malansang isda
kaya ang marapat, pagyamaning kusa
na tulad ng inang tunay na nagpala.

Ang wikang Tagalog tulad din sa Latin,
sa Ingles, Kastila, at salitang angel,
sa pagka ang Poong maalam tumingin
ang siyang nag-gawad, nagbigay sa atin.

Ang salita nati'y huad din sa iba
*na may **alfabeto** at sariling **letra**,*

na kaya nawala'y dinatnan ng sigwa
ang lunday sa lawa noong dakong una.

Joaquin's translation:

> Whenever a people truly love
> the language given them from above,
> lost freedom will they ever try
> as birds yearn for the sky.
>
> For language is a mandate sent
> to each people, country and government;
> and everyman is, like all free
> creation, born to liberty.
>
> Who does not love his own tongue is
> far worse than a brute or stinking fish,
> for we should foster and make it great
> like unto a mother blest by fate.
>
> Like Latin, English, Spanish, or speech
> of angels, Tagalog too is rich,
> for God, a wise provider, it was
> who made and handed it to us.
>
> Like the others, our language was equipped
> with its own alphabet, its own script,
> which was lost when a storm brought down in woe
> the barque on the lake long, long ago.

The last stanza of this poem is remarkable: note the reference to the Spanish conquest as a storm that wrought damage on the native culture, and led to, for example, the loss of the letters and alphabet of the indigenous language—a thesis that abounds in Rizal's later scholarly work.

Nonetheless, there has been a call to delete *Sa Aking Mga Kabata* from the list of Rizal's works, based primarily on two objections. I'll start with the most damaging.
A number of scholars have asserted that Rizal could not have authored *Sa Aking Mga Kabata*. The fly in the ointment is a crucial word in the poem: *kalayaan* – in the sense in which it is used in the second stanza, and for that matter, in the Revolution of 1896 – was not yet current in 1869!

Indeed, Rizal, by 1886, was not yet familiar with the word – as evidenced by his October 12 letter to Paciano:

> *Mi querido hermano: Allì te envoi alfin la traducciòn del Guillermo Tell de Schiller… No ignoro que està lleno de faltas que os encomiendo a tì y a mis cuñados el corregirlas: es una traducciòn casi el pie de la letra. El tagalo se me va olvidando un poco, como que no lo hablo con nadie. … Me han faltado muchos vocablos, por ejemplo para la palabra Freiheit o sea libertad; no se puede usar siempre el tagalo kaligtàsan, porque este significa que antes estuvo en alguna prisiòn, esclavitud, etc. He encontrado en la traducciòn de "El amor patrio" el nombre malayà, kalayahan que usa Marcelo del Pilar: en el ùnico libro que tengo, El Florante, no he encontrado otro nombre equivalente.* (Rizal's Correspondence with his family, Jose Rizal National Centennial Commission 1961, 256)

My dear brother,
I'm sending you at last the translation of Wilhelm Tell by Schiller… I'm aware of its many mistakes which I entrust to you and my brothers-in-law to correct. It is almost a literal translation. I'm forgetting Tagalog a little, as I don't speak it with anyone. … I lacked many words, for example, for the work *Freiheit* or liberty. The Tagalog word *kaligtasan* cannot be used, because this means that formerly he was in some prison, slavery, etc. I found in the translation of Amor Patrio the noun *malayà, kalayahan* that Marcelo H. del Pilar uses. In the only Tagalog book I have – Florante – I don't find an equivalent noun. (*Rizal-family* 1964, 243)

To my knowledge, among the first to notice the discrepancy between the 12 October 1886 letter of Rizal to Paciano and the 1869 poem, *Sa Aking Mga Kabata*, are Monsignor Moises B. Andrade and Edgar S. Yanga (from their self-published pamphlet given to the author, *Kalayaan: its birth and growth among the secular clergy of Bulacan*, 1998) and Jaime B. Veneracion (personal communication). Nilo Ocampo had likewise noted this discrepancy in his book, *May Gawa na Kaming Natapos Dini: Si Rizal at ang Wikang Tagalog* 2002, 123-24.

The 25-year old Rizal eventually used *malayà, kalayahan,* and *kalayaan* (without the h) – 55 times – in his Tagalog translation of William Tell [Guillermo Tell]. The play's relevance to the Philippine situation becomes readily apparent when Philippines is substituted for Suisa/Schwyz (Ocampo 2002, 124). Consider some telling passages:

> Tell: Ang bahay ng *kalayahan* ay itinindig sa atin ng Diyos.
> Stauffacher: *Malaya* ang taga-uisa mulang ang mundo ay mundo…
> Stauffacher: Ngunit tayong tayong tunay na lahi ng matatandang taga Schwyz, ipinaglaban nating lahi ang *kalayaan* natin.
> William Furst: Ang nasa nati'y lipulin ang sinusumpang paglupig; ang matatandang *kalayahan* na minana sa ating magugulang ay ibig natin siyang palakarin…
> Melchthal: …kaniyang palaguing ipinaglalaban ang katuiran at *kalayaan*…

For a study on Rizal's Tagalog translation of William Tell, see Ramon Guillermo's dissertation, *Das Erlöschen der Natur*: European Revolutionary Discourse in nineteenth Century Tagalog Translation (Universitat Hamburg, 2005).

Thus, it is probable that *Sa Aking Mga Kabata* was a much later fabrication—concocted perhaps by a forger during the days of Commonwealth President Manuel Luis Quezon, when Tagalog was mandated, amidst opposition from non-Tagalogs such as Ilocanos and Bisayans, to serve as the basis for the construction of a Filipino national language.

But the argument against the authenticity of *Sa Aking Mga Kabata* overlooks a crucial fact: the poem had been copied by hand several times – and had been translated to Spanish and retranslated back to Tagalog (see Nick Joaquin, *The Complete Poems and Plays of Rizal* 1976, 265). Along the way, the term "kalayaan" might have been used/inserted by later copiers or re-translators. The only way to settle this is to get hold of the original copy – sadly, this is no longer possible. The only thing we have, by way of authentication, is the testimony of Rizal's descendants – in particular Asuncion Lopez Bantug, Rizal's great grandniece, who confirms that Rizal did write *Sa Aking Mga Kabata* (see *Lolo Jose. An Intimate and Illustrated Portrait of Rizal*, 2nd edition, Vibal Foundation and Intramuros Administration 2008, 19)

The testimony of a Rizal descendant, however, does not constitute 100% proof that the 8-year old Rizal did compose *Sa Aking Mga Kabata*. Indeed the poem could very well be a 20th century fabrication, possibly during the time of Pres. Quezon.

The likelihood that *Sa Aking Mga Kabata* was a much later fabrication does not, however, render it worthless. The value of the poem lies in the fact that it testifies to the influence of Rizal's historical perspective on subsequent Filipino nationalist writers, and even forgers.

The lineaments of Rizal's nationalist historical perspective may be traced from *Junto Al Pasig*, a play written by an 18-year old Rizal, to El Amor Patrio, written in 1882, which Bonifacio rendered in 1896 into his poem "Pag-Ibig sa Tinubuang Lupa" (popularized into a haungtingly beautiful song by Inang Laya), to Rizal's 1890 annotations to

Morga's *Sucesos de las Islas Filipinas*, and, finally, to his 1896 untitled farewell poem (posthumously given the title *Mi Ultimo Adios*), now considered among the all-time greatest 1,000 poems in the Spanish Language (see *Mil Mejores Poesias De La Lengua Castellana*, edited by J. Bergua).

Remarkably, all of these are prefigured in *Sa Aking Mga Kabata*. For this reason alone, the poem should not be dismissed simply because of its questioned provenance.

The second argument raised against the authenticity of "Sa Aking Mga Kabata" is that the 8-year old Rizal could not have been capable of conceiving the ideas expressed in the poem. This is most unfair. History abounds in child prodigies who have composed or created something notable at a very early age. To cite just three:

Maria Gaetana Agnesi, the beautiful Italian mathematician, wrote her first book at the age of nine. She spoke fluent French, Greek, Hebrew, Spanish, German and Latin by age 11.

Wolfgang Amadeus Mozart composed his first piece of published music at age 5. By his teenage years, he had already composed many concertos, sonatas, operas and symphonies.

Sor Juana Inés de la Cruz of Mexico was writing religious poetry at age 8, and had taught herself Latin as a child. By her adolescence, she knew Greek logic and learned an Aztec language called Nahuatl.

Why would it be incredible that Rizal could write a Tagalog poem at age 8? Why can't we accept Rizal as a child prodigy?

Given the facts I've cited, I leave it to my dear readers to decide for themselves whether Rizal really wrote the wonderful poem *Sa Aking Mga Kabata*.

Part III
RIZAL AND SOCIETY

The Political Ideas of Jose Rizal

Belinda A. Aquino, PhD

FIRST OF ALL, I would like to thank the Knights of Rizal and the Philippine Cultural Foundation for giving me this opportunity to articulate some thoughts about our national hero, Dr. Jose Rizal, on this auspicious occasion marking the 128th anniversary of his birthday. This is especially significant to me personally because the Rizal contest is one of my farewell activities in Hawaii. In a few days, I will be leaving, not permanently, I hope, this beautiful land of aloha, which has been home to me for the past 19 years, to take up a new job at the University of the Philippines. That job incidentally will find me in future occasions such as this in the Philippines, where the life and death of Jose Rizal have become part of the lasting cultural traditions of our country.

As with all great heroes of history, Rizal's most enduring legacy to the world and to Filipinos in particular is timelessness. One hundred twenty-eight years after his birth, he is still very much alive. His statue at Luneta has become the symbol of the Philippines. He is on practically all aspects of our culture – books, art, theater, artifacts, even on matchboxes. He has become an integral part of the national psyche, a part of the reality of Filipino life. By executing him in 1896, the Spaniards made him live forever.

The stuff of legend usually consists of achievement that transcends the capacity of ordinary mortals. And in this regard, Rizal was an extremely extraordinary person: he was a genius. He was a doctor, a scientist, a novelist, a writer, a poet, an essayist, an artist, a linguist, and just about everything else you could imagine. His genius included anticipating changes in the Philippines a hundred years from his time. He wrote *Filipinas Dentro de Cien Años* (The Philippines A Century Hence) in four parts for *La Solidaridad*, the organ of the Philippine revolutionary movement in Spain between September 1889 and January 1890.

Being a political scientist by training, I would like to dwell for a moment on the political ideas of Rizal because it was precisely his politics that set him in trouble with the Spanish authorities in the remaining two decades of the 19th century. He could have opted to be content and comfortable as a doctor, or as a literary person. Many Filipino leaders of his generation did just that. They chose not to rock the boat. They collaborated with the ruling powers, namely the Spaniards and their cohorts. But Rizal went several steps beyond in pursuit of his political ideals. The starting point of Rizal's vision for his country was the situation in the Philippines at the time. According to the late Jesuit scholar, Father Horacio de la Costa, that situation called for a fundamental change in the relationship which had hitherto obtained between the colony and the mother country, Spain in this case. In short, between the dominant and subject people. In order for that change to occur, it was necessary for Filipinos themselves to understand the causes that produced the situation. Spanish rule was imposed on the Philippines by force of conquest. Before that, Filipinos had their own history, their own culture. They had fairly sophisticated forms of social and economic organization. They were governed by indigenous rulers under native laws. They were free to worship their own gods. They had their own alphabet and languages. They had various forms of native literature. To cut a long story short, the Spaniards came and wiped out all that. They imposed an alien culture. The Filipinos were overwhelmed by the superior forces of Spain. In the words of De la Costa again, "they lost confidence in their past, faith in the present, hope in their future." The native Filipinos were uprooted from their birthright, their cultural heritage. Little by little, they neglected their ancient traditions and forgot their past. The Filipinos remained in this state of subjection for three centuries, an awfully long time. That was the saddest part of Filipino history. That was the story of colonialism.

Rizal, in his various writings, constantly enjoined his fellow Filipinos to understand the roots of their oppression, and to resist it. This was precisely his point in his ringing declaration, *"There are no tyrants where there are no slaves!"* That is a truism for all time. Today, we say it takes two to tango. Filipinos had to be awakened from centuries of repression, stupor, darkness. In short, they had to be jolted into thinking of themselves as a nation. Heretofore, they were fragmented by regional, ethnic, geographic, class and other kinds of barriers in a situation that could be characterized as a feudal system. Rizal wanted them to be conscious as Filipinos, not as Tagalogs or Ilocanos or Visayans. And that was more than a century ago. He was really ahead of his time.

Now, Rizal placed his last hope on the Filipino youth who would become the leaders of future generations. In this year's Rizal Essay Contest, we thought we would emphasize that theme. Rizal exhorted the youth to pursue the goal of education. He was after all, a man of arts and letters who nurtured the intellectual life. What he wanted the youth to do was reflected in the themes of his novels, *Noli Me Tangere* and *El Filibusterismo*. Freedom could not be obtained, he said, in a climate of ignorance and apathy. And education would not be enough either. The exercise of freedom presupposes a long and arduous process of self-discipline. That was his lasting message to the youth of the land.

The larger political concept that Rizal espoused was nationalism. What did he mean by that? It was not an elaborate new-fangled concept; nor was it seditious as the Spaniards interpreted it. He simply meant the capacity for sacrifice, the ability to forego personal needs and private motives for the welfare of the people and the good of the nation. De la Costa interprets it as *"Sin dudas, sin pesar."* That is to say, without thinking twice about it and without calculating the cost. In the end, Rizal made the ultimate sacrifice. He gave up his own life. His martyrdom sparked the spirit of revolutionary nationalism among Filipinos that culminated in the Philippine revolution of 1896.

This in brief constitutes Rizal's political ideas, which remain relevant today as all kinds of violence and oppression continue to mark modern political systems. The conditions he talked about then are still true today.

But if Rizal were alive today, he would be very proud of the Filipino youth in Hawaii. More and more of them are pursuing higher aspirations. When I first came to Hawaii in the 60s as a student, there were hardly any Filipino students or American students of Filipino ancestry. Today, while they are not yet coming to the university in great numbers, their presence is definitely established. So much so that when the Center for Philippine Studies put out an announcement for audition for a *sarsuwela* to be staged this weekend at Kennedy Theater, many of them appeared. The cast of 40 is three-fourths Filipino-American – they could be your sons, daughters, nephews, nieces or other relatives. You too would be extremely proud of them. I did not mean to end on a commercial, but if you come out and watch the *sarsuwela* which starts on Friday, you will be reminded of Jose Rizal as the young actors, circa 1907, start one of their songs with a fervent *"To Free a Nation!"*

As I leave Hawaii, I am comforted by the thought that you will continue to keep alive the genius of Rizal. I hope to keep in touch with you regarding your future Rizal related activities. Perhaps as next year's theme, you should think of Rizal and Filipino women. He wrote a beautiful piece called "Letter to the Women of Malolos."

This should also be a signal to you in the Knights of Rizal to extend your membership to women. On with the times! Thank you and Mabuhay.

(Remarks by Dr. Belinda Aquino, founding Director of the Center for Philippine Studies, as guest speaker of Program on Awarding the Winners of the 1989 Rizal Essay Contest and 128th Birth Anniversary of Dr. Jose Rizal, Hale Koa Hotel, June 19, 1989.)

Reconciling Faith and Reason

Sir Elihu A. Ybañez, LL.B, KGCR

Diplomats, Trustees of the Supreme Council, fellow knights, and honored guests:

I would like to thank the Knights of Rizal Arizona and Las Vegas Chapters for hosting this conference. I am truly honored to be standing in front of you, an assemblage of individuals suffused with Dr. Jose P. Rizal's ideals.

Two months ago, I solemnly took my oath as your Supreme Commander. Inspired by your charge, I affirmed my commitment to lead this Order with courage, compassion, character, and most of all, fidelity to the ideals of Dr. Jose P. Rizal.

Fellow knights and brothers, foremost among our concerns must be to bind the wounds of division and lay to rest our bickering, petty rivalries, distrust, and suspicions that have dissipated our time and energy. The overriding principle we must establish is that we seek consensus and recognize dissent, but we uphold common discipline like a trained and dedicated army, and we respect leadership – not undermine it.

In this spirit, I ask that we view this organization afresh and I invite you to move forward with me. To borrow the words of Dr. Jose P. Rizal, *"We, therefore, profess, gentlemen, once again unity and solidarity among us. The good and welfare of our country is our motive."*[1] Let us heed his advice that, *"The spirit of tolerance ought to prevail. In discussions, the conciliatory tendency ought to dominate before the tendency to oppose."*[2]

We must, therefore, summon the harmony and cooperation we need because we have one common ground to work from: Jose Rizal's aspiration for the Motherland. It is only by concord and collective action that we can realize the highest of our hopes for this Order and the Filipino nation, and so, I trust in your fealty. With your support, we will construct a 35-storey building as our International Headquarters and start the drive to build the Knights of Rizal Museum. These projects are consistent with our status as the sole order of knighthood in the Philippines and our vision of a perfect union among Filipinos in honoring the memory and teachings of Dr. Jose P. Rizal.

We will launch a Knights of Rizal coffee table book on February 22, 2019 at our international conference in Antipolo City. A team of professional writers has been commissioned by the Supreme Council for this project. An active supporter of the Order will provide the professional fees of the writers so we will only shoulder the cost of printing. The coffee table book will be like an open window to the soul of the Order for all to see. It is hoped that the unique blend of images and information will inspire conversation, immerse the reader, and promote the Order.

The coffee table book is a great step in building our brand. In the 21st century, branding – the perception that people have when they hear or think of a business or an organization – is important in creating greater social impact and tighter organizational cohesion. It is said that if you don't go online, you will get left behind. As the world has changed into a digital arena, we have tapped the power of social media. Additionally, we will put up our official website to increase our visibility, share the uniqueness of the Order, and clearly deliver our message to the youth – the millennials and the emerging generation, iGen – who do not just use technology but integrate it into their lives flawlessly. The website will be an invaluable and always available resource for information and communication.

We will expand the reach of our organization and increase its impact through a strong program of recruiting quality members to join the Order and reviving chapters with dwindling membership. We will add other priorities as ideas emerge and as we make progress in the coming months. Your input is always welcome and I commit to maintain a transparent dialogue with you.

Much of what has been written about Rizal focuses on his political thinking and achievements. Rizal, however, did not just study society and searched for knowledge; he also tried to reconcile faith and reason.

The enduring greatness of Dr. Jose P. Rizal lies in the nobility of his conviction that real faith consists of purity of thoughts and clean behavior, charity, justice, and a creed based on equality and freedom. According to Rizal, charity is the greatest of all the virtues because it inclines us to love God above all things for His own sake, and our neighbors for the sake of God.[3]

Rizal's life-mission was working for liberty, justice, human dignity, and recognition of the rights of Filipino men and women. He also stressed that Filipino mothers should teach their children love of God and raise them close to the image of God - the God who is the Father of all; the God who does not fatten on the blood of the poor, who does not rejoice at the plaints of the afflicted and does not obfuscate the intelligent mind.[4] Rizal likewise reminded women that faith is not merely reciting prayers and wearing religious pictures but living the real Christian way with good morals.[5] Indeed, he was a torchbearer for love of God characterized by reasoned faith; he gave light to others so they would discern their own way.

In one of Rizal's essays, he described love of country as passion that *"is never effaced once it has penetrated the heart, because it carries with it a divine stamp"*, *"the most powerful force behind the most sublime actions"*, and *"of all love. . . is the greatest, the most heroic and the most disinterested"*. He wrote about the Motherland for whom *"some have sacrificed their youth, their pleasures. . . others their blood; all have died bequeathing to their Motherland*

. . . liberty and glory."[6]

With tenacity, Rizal used his writing skills to move a whole country to free itself. Under his leadership, the Reform or Propaganda Movement, as it became known, flourished. It triumphed, not in the sense that it attained its goals of obtaining parliamentary representation for the Filipinos, but in its fruits. Other youths followed in Rizal's footsteps and fought for separation which ultimately led to our independence.[7]

Rizal decided that love of country should supplant all other considerations, even that of his family or his own, as he remained faithful to his muse and his cause: the Motherland and her freedom.[8] And so, a nation was born out of the ashes of his sacrifices.

Integrity was a hallmark of Rizal's life. Even his scientific studies were marked by an attempt to be as objective and honest in his findings as he could muster. His moral compass led him to insist that the Propaganda be as factual as was possible and encouraged the writers to stop using pen names but their own so that people could judge their writings with a real and not imagined author.

When he was exiled in Dapitan, officials hinted that he might escape if he wished but no man on earth could persuade him to do what he considered dishonorable.[9]

In a letter *"to the Filipinos"* dated June 20, 1892, he stated that: *"I cannot go on living knowing that so many suffer unjust persecution because of me ... I also want to show those who deny our patriotism that we know how to die doing our duty and for our convictions. What does death matter if one dies for what one loves, for one's country and loved ones?"*[10]

He also wrote: *"I am ready to serve my country not only with the pen but also with my life whenever my country would demand of me this sacrifice. . . and God could ask me, why did you not combat the evil and injustice when you saw them?"*[11]

For his people, Rizal was ready to give up everything for he knew, with a certainty that only the truly honorable and brave can ever have, that his ideas were correct and would trounce the forces of oppression that overwhelmed his Motherland. This strong sense of purpose and his tenacity remind me of a verse in the Bible. Micah 6:8 instructs: *"The LORD God has told us what is right and what He demands: 'See that justice is done, let mercy be your first concern, and humbly obey your God.'"*

May we, like Dr. Jose P. Rizal, profess our love of God by being relentless in loving our country and by committing to the welfare of others.

Dr. Jose P. Rizal provided all of us a very rich legacy as he embodied and realized the best of what a Filipino can be. It is only fitting to look once again at the way he lived his life to be inspired to move forward for ourselves and for this Order, and to finish what he began: the formation of a nation where every Filipino is truly discerning and free.

It is our bounden duty as knights to exemplify and demand a high standard of conduct from our associates and country-men, and to inculcate Rizal's ethical values in our youth by opening their eyes to the possibilities enabled by education and virtuous leadership. By our example, let us show them the kind of potential that each of them has. It is not enough for us to just go through the motions or to just show up at our meetings. Integrity, our commitment to uprightness in both our personal and professional lives, the morals we up-hold daily, and the level to which we follow them will deter-mine our credibility. It is important that knights, starting with each one of us in this assembly, serve as role models in our communities. We want the good that Rizal demon-strated to last not just here, not just for us, but everywhere, for everyone, for future generations. When we lead and serve like Rizal, and motivate others to do the same, we can be sure that the challenges to our strength as a nation would have been surpassed and the Philippines will thrive as one of the best countries in the whole world.

How many of the youth you inspire and how many lives you touch depend on your enthusiasm, your dedication, and your openness to new ideas.

The challenge for us is to empower every knight to truly embrace and typify what this Order is about, to recognize what doors it opens, and to understand the privilege of being a steward of Rizal's vision and aspirations. We need to assume leadership for building stronger chapters, and that starts with bringing in new members.

Membership is our job, it's every knight's opportunity. We need to find those men who are waiting to be asked and find the people who never thought about the Order. And if they say yes and they become members, we need to mentor them and make sure that they find a meaningful role in the organization.

Furthermore, we need to work on bringing in younger members to ensure that Rizal's love of God, love of country, integrity, and wealth of wisdom will be passed on to those who will eventually become the leaders and influencers of tomorrow. If we want to attract younger members, we have to think about what life is like for them and promote the relevance of Rizal's ideas.

We have a lot of work to do if we are to demonstrate clear value and contemporary appeal to the global marketplace. Every one of us here and everyone who made the commitment to take a leadership role must ask ourselves: What will make the Order more attractive and more viable? What makes the Order unique? What will make it an organization I can be truly proud of? These are the things that I want us to reflect on and share.

When knights get engaged, values change. Then we'll have

given the Philippines and the world a gift that lasts and transforms. For this reason, let us endeavor to make Rizal's teachings known to the world by leveraging our strengths into the ability to make an impact. And let the words of Dr. Jose P. Rizal strengthen our resolve, *"Let us then put our trust in God and in the sincerity of our purposes."*[12]

Allow me to conclude this address with a prayer. *"May the Lord establish the work of our hands and may He make our endeavors successful"* (Psalm 90:17).

Thank you!

End Notes

[1] Jose Rizal to his mother, 1885.

[2] Manuel Quintal. "The Universality of Rizal's Ideas and Its Relevance to Filipinos Today".
Taukappaphi.com. http://www.taukappaphi.com/articles/the-universality-of-rizals-ideas-and-itsrelevance-to-filipinos-today/ [Date Accessed: February 23, 2018].

[3] University of Rizal System. "Rizal's Moral Legacies for Our Daily Life". SlideShare.
https://www.slideshare.net/jjcziamae/rizals-moral-legacies-for-our-daily-life [Date Accessed: July 31, 2018].

[4] Edwin D. Bael. "Rizal – Nobility of Filipinos". Blogspot. htttp://rizalsignificance.blogspot.com/2010/06/rizal-nobility-of-filipinos.html [Date Accessed:
August 01, 2018].

[5] Dimasalang Laong Laan. "Rizal's Intellectual Legacies in Selected Essays". WordPress.
https://dimasalanglaonglaan.wordpress.com/rizals-intellectual-legacies-in-selected-essays/ [Date
Accessed: July 31, 2018].

[6] Ma. Cielito G. Reyno. "For Love of Country". National Historical Commission of the Philippines.
http://nhcp.gov.ph/for-love-of-country/ [Date Accessed: July 31, 2018].

[7] *Ibid.*

[8] *Ibid.*

[9] Dr. Robert L. Yoder. "Rizal on Honesty". Blogspot. http://laonlaan .blogspot.com/2008/10/rizalon-honesty.html [Date Accessed: August 01, 2018].

[10] Torn and Frayed in Manila. "Jose Rizal: The Man Who Refused to Give Up His Reason". Typepad. http://tornandfrayed.typepad.com/tornandfrayed/2009/03/jose-rizal-the-man-who-refused-togive-up-his-reason.html [Date Accessed: August 01, 2018].

[11] Ma. Cielito G. Reyno. "Timeless Lessons from Rizal". National Historical Commission of the Philippines. http://nhcp.gov.ph/timeless-lessons-from-rizal/ [Date Accessed: August 01, 2018].

[12] Jose Rizal to his mother, 1885.

Foundations of Rizalian Leadership

Sir Serafin Colmenares Jr., PhD, KGCR

According to the Institute for Educational Leadership, leadership is a process, both internal and external, that leads to (1) the ability to analyze one's own strengths and weaknesses, set goals, and have the self-esteem, confidence, motivation, and abilities to carry them out; and (2) the ability to guide or direct others on a course of action, influence their opinion and behavior, and serve as a role model.

Some leaders are born. Others are made. Most are both. But all have certain qualities or characteristics that make them good leaders. Rizal was one of them.

Leadership qualities refer to those attributes, internal or external, that characterize good leaders. These qualities can be developed or may be naturally part of their personality. Some of these qualities may stand out as being more important than the others.

Sir Pablo Trillana III, past Supreme Commander of the Knights of Rizal, tells us that *"Rizal's life is a study on the principles of leadership."* Rizal has not given us a written guide as to what he thinks leadership should be, nor has he given us a list of what attributes a leader should have. He has, however, given us his writings and his life from which we can glean the leadership qualities which he espoused and exhibited. He not only wrote about them; he lived them. Although he himself did not serve in a leadership position, he provided organizational, intellectual, moral, and community leadership, and was recognized as a leader, not only by his compatriots in Europe but by the Filipino people themselves.

Foundations of Leadership

Based on Rizal's various written works and his own life's example, becoming a leader in the Rizalian mold involves the development of what may be called the foundations, or the building blocks of leadership. There are three of them.

Character

The first is **character**. Character refers to who you are, your values and attributes. It refers to your internal qualities. What are the character traits that define a good leader? Dr. Pablo Trillana III, in an article published in the *Philippine Daily Inquirer* issue dated January 4, 2011, identifies six of them:

One is vision. A leader should have a clear idea of where he or she is going. Without a clear goal, all planned moves will fail. As a well-known author on leadership said, *"everyone can steer the ship, but it takes a leader to chart the course."*

Rizal was a visionary. His goal was the achievement of Filipino nationhood, something he had nurtured from childhood and pursued passionately in his adult years until his death. His works, *Noli Me Tangere* and *El Filibusterismo*, expressed his patriotic sentiments, and the five points of his La Liga Filipina spelled out what he wanted to see in the Philippines.

Second is trustworthiness. Trust refers to a firm reliance on the integrity, ability, dependability, reliability, or character of a person. People follow when they believe in a leader, when they trust or have confidence in him or her. To be trusted, a leader must be transparent and honest in his actions. A leader is true to his or her word and not duplicitous. He or she must lead by example. This is necessary to get the buy-in from his or her followers and to show the leader's worth.

Rizal has proven his worth, he made his life a building

block, a useful stone, a role model. He earned the trust of his countrymen and they believed and followed him. He not only was a chosen leader of the Filipino expatriate community in Spain; he was also made honorary president of the Katipunan, even if he did not adhere to its revolutionary aims.

Third is <u>altruism</u>. A leader looks at the big picture. He or she is not self-centered and does not work for selfish aims or for the benefit of a few. His or her goal is always the good of the greater number.

For Rizal, the goal was the good of the Filipino people and the well-being of the country. In 1896, he said: *"In my heart I have suppressed all loves, except that of my native land; in my mind I have erased all ideas which do not signify her progress; and my lips have forgotten the names of the native races in the Philippines in order not to say more than Filipinos."*

Fourth is <u>open-mindedness</u>. A leader should not have a one-track mind; he or she should be able to explore and be open to alternative solutions to problems. A leader should be flexible, not self-righteous; a leader listens to other points of view. He or she must be open to and welcome criticism and not be vindictive. Prejudice or bias do not make a good leader.

Rizal mapped out not one but several roads toward national redemption. He was a pacifist and favored reforms, but he did not completely dismiss armed revolution if the people were prepared and ready for it. These themes ran through the *Noli Me Tangere* and the *El Filibusterismo*. His *La Liga Filipina* was another attempt to establish a reformed society in the Philippines.

Fifth is <u>sacrifice</u>. A leader must be willing to suffer and sacrifice. He or she must be willing to forfeit or relinquish something in exchange for, or for the sake of, something of greater value.

In the *El Filibusterismo*, Simoun asked Padre Florentino what must be done while the country is still under the shackles of a colonial power. Padre Florentino answered: *"Sufrir y trabajar."* Endure and work. To build the Filipino nation, Rizal emphasized the need to sacrifice, to go the extra mile so that the cherished goal may be achieved. He said: *"victory is the child of struggle, joy blossoms from suffering, and redemption is the product of sacrifice."* And he willingly gave the supreme sacrifice of dying for his county.

Sixth is <u>virtue, or moral force</u>. A leader must be ethical and morally upright.

For Rizal, the building of a nation requires good men who must be virtuous. What is virtue? According to Rizal, true virtue is modest and simple: *"to do good to one's fellowmen, to make a sacrifice for the happiness of others, to tell the truth even to one's detriment, to look upon all as brothers..."* He also defined it as the *"habitual performance of duty,"* indicating that leaders should not only be aware of their duties but should perform them to the best of their ability. As a student in Madrid, Rizal served as a moralist to his fellow Filipinos – according to V.G. Sinco (*Jose Rizal: Reminiscences and Travels, 2011*), he *"urged his fellow students to attend their classes regularly, to refrain from gambling and wasting away the precious time of their youth, and to bear constantly in their minds their parents' sacrifices and their duty to the land of their birth."* Indeed, as one writer said, *"what the country needs are men and women with moral, rather than political, authority; individuals who fight for justice, not power; who do not only create wealth but ensure its equitable distribution; who respect heritage; who transcend nationalism and are accepting of other faiths and culture."* Rizal urged his countrymen to live a life of virtue. For him, without virtue there is no liberty, without virtue there is no redemption.

Having a clear vision, trustworthiness, concern for the greater good, open-mindedness, willingness to sacrifice, and being moral and virtuous – all these character traits provide a solid grounding or foundation for all who aspire for leadership. Always remember that leadership springs from within – it is about who you are as much as what you do.

Competence

The second leadership foundation is **competence.** Competence is the ability to perform a specific role. Competence encompasses your intellectual capacity, your skills and knowledge, your technical expertise.

All of us have our own chosen field of expertise. But as leaders, we need to go beyond the knowledge we have accumulated in the field we have chosen. We need to learn and develop other competencies that would help us become effective leaders. The following are some areas of competency that leaders need to develop:

Communication – this includes public speaking/writing, and engaging the participation of others

Teamwork – this means respecting others, performing roles of both leader and follower, building on strengths, and commitment to free group input and expression

Responsibility – this means doing your job, understanding one's role in the community, pride in being a member of a larger group, and taking responsibility for one's actions and the resulting consequences

Professionalism – this means demonstrating tactfulness, understanding protocols, acting appropriately in a given context, delivering quality work, and positively presenting oneself to others

Project Management – this includes setting goals/developing action steps, implementation, meeting facilitation, and evaluation

In addition, as Rizalian leaders and as leaders of the Knights of Rizal, we should not only be knowledgeable about Rizal and his works; we should also be knowledgeable about our organization and how it works, particularly its bylaws and the rules that govern it. It would also help if officers are familiar with Robert's Rules of Order, if commanders/deputy commanders know how to preside and facilitate meetings, if pursuivants know how to take and write meeting minutes, if exchequers know how to prepare financial reports, and if chancellors know how to conduct rituals.

Competencies may be developed through education, training, coaching, observations, travel and reading.

"Mag-aral ka," advised Elias to Basilio in the *Noli Me Tangere.* Study, acquire knowledge, be enlightened – such was Rizal's message to Filipinos, because he believed that it is through education that an individual is enabled to fully develop him/herself and become a contributing member to society; it is through education that one becomes free. Rizal developed his competencies through education – locally and abroad – and became knowledgeable and skillful in various fields. He read a lot and trained under renowned experts. Through his travels, he became a keen observer of the places and peoples he visited.

Action

The third foundation that leaders need to develop is in the realm of **action.** This refers to one's ability to take the initiative, to communicate, to lead by example, and to achieve, or apply and carry out decisions. It is the application of what you know and what you want to do. It is *"walking the talk."* As the saying goes, *"leadership is action, not position".*

A leader must be able to adapt and make decisive decisions. A leader must not only have the courage to initiate things and to focus on the task in hand but also have the will to pursue them to fruition. Furthermore, leadership includes the ability to give way, to let go and not cling to power. While a leader may think that he or she is the best for the job, there might be other people who are as good or even better than him or her. A leader knows how to develop other leaders and make them shine.

Rizal was an action-oriented leader. He not only talked, wrote about, and initiated things, but he pursued them to fruition despite difficulties. He persevered to finish his two novels in the face of cold, hunger and the lack of funds. He wanted reforms, and he wrote, fought and died for it. And he was humble enough to let others take over the leadership position he occupies. He said: *"My most ardent desire is that…six or seven Filipinos should grow to overshadow me so completely that no one would even remember me."*

How did Rizal develop and show his leadership skills? Rizal's preparation for leadership was done through study, travel, writing, organizing, and initiating and implementing projects. From a young age he delved into the study of various subjects – from history to literature, to art and philosophy, to medicine, engineering and the natural sciences, etc. – to develop his competencies. He travelled around the world to learn about foreign cultures, the better to understand his own. He wanted to learn as much as he could so he can have a broader and open-minded view of everything around him. He was especially interested in the history not only of the Philippines but that of the world, and he believed that in order to know and understand other peoples, it is necessary to learn their languages. He thus became a linguist and developed an understanding of other cultures by traveling to Europe, Asia and America – not only because he wanted to compare his country with other countries but also because he wanted to project his people and culture to others. Rizal did not study just for knowledge's sake; he applied and made good use of the knowledge he gained.

He used his pen to provide intellectual and moral leadership to his countrymen – forming the triumvirate (with Graciano Lopez-Jaena and Marcelo del Pilar) that published the *La Solidaridad*, the mouthpiece of the reform movement – writing a host of essays and articles such as The Indolence of the Filipino, The Philippines a Century Hence, Letter to the Women of Malolos, etc., and annotated Morga's *Sucesos de las Islas Filipinas*, all of which exposed the situation in the Philippines. His two novels, the *Noli Me Tangere* and *El Filibusterismo*, planted the seed for the Philippine revolution against Spain.

He organized and joined organizations, not to gain positions or for personal gain, but to advance his goal of a better Philippines – forming the *Kidlat Club* to make Filipinos know each other during the Paris Exposition in 1889, and the *Indios Bravos* to defend the honor of Filipinos abroad. He was a member of the *Circulo Hispano-Filipino* and was one of the organizers of the *La Solidaridad*, the mouthpiece of Filipino expatriates in Spain. He also joined Freemasonry, believing in its principles of liberty, equality and fraternity, and as a tool to liberate his people.

He organized the still-born North Borneo agricultural colony project, with him as leader of the planters. He also formed the ill-fated *La Liga Filipina*, a civic society which tried to provide a blueprint for a Filipino nation. Foiled in his attempts by the Spanish authorities, he somehow was able to implement some of his plans by providing community leadership during his exile in Dapitan, where he founded a farmers' cooperative, established a school, provided volunteer medical services, and engaged in various community development projects.

It is of interest to note that Rizal never actually served in a position in the organizations he joined or formed, although he was, without doubt, the recognized leader of Filipinos in Spain and in the Philippines. He was offered, once, the leadership position of the Filipino community in Spain but he declined in order to preserve the unity of the group.

Conclusion

In short, leadership begins with what the leader must be, that is, the values and principles that shape a leader's character. Skills are those things you know how to do, your competence in everything from the technical side of your job to the people skills and other competencies a leader requires to be effective. But character and competence, while necessary, are not enough. You cannot be an effective leader until you apply what you know, until you act and do what you must.

Leadership thus rests upon the development of three building blocks – character, competence, and action. To become a leader, one must develop all three. Rizal developed and exhibited these in his life and in his works. Now let us ask ourselves, as leaders of our respective communities, and as leaders of this august institution – which of these leadership building blocks do we have and which of these we don't? What areas do we need to work on?

Our organization needs the best minds and the best leaders its membership has to offer. This is because we, as leaders, have the responsibility to write the current and the next chapters of the history of our organization. But we cannot simply write them – we must make sure these chapters are worth reading.

Thank you.

Speech given during the 7th USA Regional Assembly of the Knights of Rizal held on August 31-September 2, 2018 in Las Vegas, Nevada.

Touch Me: An Invitation to Critical and Constructive Awareness and Rizalism

Sir Raymund Llanes Liongson, PhD, KGCR

RIZALIAN BROTHERS ALL, good afternoon.

At a banquet of Filipino students held at Café de Madrid on December 31, 1883, Dr. Jose Rizal proclaimed: "In my heart, I have suppressed all loves except that of my motherland."

And writing to his mother in early 1885, he penned: "The best legacy that parents can leave to their children is an upright judgment, generosity in the exercise of our rights, and perseverance in adversity. And a son pays the greatest honor to his parents with his **integrity** and good name; let the son never make his [parents] tremble with indignation or with shame . . ."

I was tasked to focus my talk on "Rizal's Legacy: Love of Country and Integrity" – a component of the theme of this year's Regional biennial assembly – and the preceding quotes from Dr. Rizal capture and reflect his unwavering commitments to these virtues: Love of Country and Integrity.

We have always assumed that the first legacy is evident and clear. To native born citizens, that country decidedly refers to the land of birth. But to immigrants, children of immigrants, people of mixed races and nationalities, refugees and exiles, that country can be ambiguous. Are we referring to the Philippines, the U.S., Canada, or even China? What happens when the ancestral country gets in conflict with the birth or adoptive country? I leave those provocative moral and political questions for your reflection.

Rizal became a crusader for his country's freedom. He decided that love of country should supplant all other considerations, even that of his family or his own.

Rizal saw the many injustices suffered by his fellow Filipinos: they depended on the religious corporations or on big landowners, for a land to till, or for a living; people had misgivings in airing their grievances or protesting against the friars or the government, fearing agonizing retaliations from them. In short, there was no real freedom of the press or speech. Most Filipinos lacked the privilege of education and its resultant benefits, or if they did have education, this was the obscurantist kind generally propagated by the colonialist policy, which not only kept Filipinos in the dark about their rights, but had molded them into an abject, submissive people ignorant or ashamed of their own heritage – a heritage that existed even before the arrival of the Spaniards. Rizal realized that the Philippines had not been consistently represented in the Spanish parliament. For him, this has resulted in injustice, or of being deprived of their basic rights.

Love and service of country requires that we understand the situation of the land and its people. In his essay "The Indolence of the Filipino People," Rizal wrote: "We can only serve our country by telling her the truth, however bitter it be."

And so, let us once more expose today's social cancer "on the steps of the temple," to borrow Rizal's phrase, so that anyone who can make the proper diagnosis can offer the proper prescription and intervention.

Back home, poverty remains to be the mother of all social ills. About half of the population live in poverty, while five percent (over 5 million) have no source of livelihood. Tens of thousands have resorted to drugs as a way to escape their poverty and miserable plight. Over ten percent of the population has to leave in order to live, many of them paying a costly social price such as the painful separation from family, abuse and humiliation of their dignity, if not loss of dear life.

Brute power and corruption, ignorance and indifference, falsehoods and manipulations continue to assault democratic freedom.

Human rights have become a devalued currency with thousands getting killed – some of them at very young ages – without the due process of the law. If Rizal and his fictional character Crispin were to be announced killed today, one would readily guess why: *"dahil nanlaban o nagtangkang tumakas."* Meanwhile, human rights advocates are undermined and threatened. Even international human rights monitors and bodies are not spared.

Vulgar language and public humiliation are cheered and celebrated by mindless audience and sycophants. *'Tang ina* has become as casual as *kumusta ka*. And those who chastise degrading language are either *"gago", "bugok",* or simply "not have a sense of humor."

Denigration of women – especially those who can muster their courage and intellectual prowess – also continues to rise. Misogynism has become a political weapon for some men who are in power, threatened by the rising popularity and collective strength of women.

Political dynasties have become the rule in the determination of leadership and allocation of power. This system has limited world-views, compromised check-and-balances, and facilitated corruption.

Cheap-minded and unprincipled political turncoats or *balimbings* swiftly jump from their party to another to preserve themselves and their powers.

Critics and dissenters are vilified and punished. Some are harassed by legal actions, others have been booted out from their posts. In some cases, critics now find themselves behind bars. The less fortunate ones have been laid to rest six feet under.

Critical press and media are likewise under attack, outrageously labeled as "destabilizers" and dismissed as a source of "fake news", thus justifying their takeover or attempt to revoke their license to operate.

Meanwhile, a cunning Goliathan Dragon power disrespectfully tramples the country's sacred zones – its Exclusive Economic Zones and Continental Shelves – and those mandated to protect them offer excuses for the egregious acts. Those in power have become timid in asserting the country's territory and sovereignty, recognizing only a dubious friendship and hollow assurances.

And the litany of societal ills can go on and on.

What is then our role in the country's yearning for change and reform? How should citizens respond to their recurring ills and pains?

For us who have transplanted ourselves in foreign soils, how do we take part in addressing some of the foregoing issues?

In his correspondence with fellow reformists, Rizal candidly wrote:

> "If our countrymen are counting on us here in Europe, they are very much mistaken…The battlefield is the Philippines: There is where we should meet…there we will help one another, there together we will suffer or triumph perhaps. The majority of our compatriots in Europe are afraid, they flee from the fire, and they are brave only so long as they are in a peaceful country! The Philippines should not count on them; she should

depend on her own strength."

Rizal's words continue to reverberate in our ears, shaking our consciousness. This is a tough challenge for many of us. This reminds me of an interview I had with a University of Hawaii Ethnic Studies chair and professor, Dr. Dean Alegado, who resigned from his job to be able to go back to the Philippines and work there. When I asked what made him decide to go back when everyone is trying to migrate out of the country for greener pasture, he responded: "That is not the question. The question is 'when are you going back?' His response still haunts me in my sleep to these days.

IN THE "LAND OF THE FREE AND HOME OF THE BRAVE," we continue to witness racism and discrimination of colored people, immigrants, refugees, women, believers of other faiths, and free thinkers. Violence against colored people (such as racial profiling, assault and murder) committed by agents of the government is becoming a norm. Free press and media have been described as "the enemy of the people" and citizens are urged to "not believe" what they see. Placing legalities and technicalities over humanity and compassion, children are heartlessly separated from their parents. Walls are built instead of human bridges. Meanwhile, it has not secured itself from the external attack of its most sacred democratic institutions – elections.

We have serious societal ills and challenges and we must respond accordingly. As they say, "the only thing necessary for the triumph of evil is for good men to do nothing."

Love of country is not "my country, right or wrong;" but "if my country is right, we keep it right; if wrong, we set it right."

And so here we are – the Knights of Rizal, in shining armor of truth, freedom, excellence, rectitude, and honorable character, the Rizalian traits that we profess we embrace and possess.

And our ability to stand and live by our claimed ideals is what we call **integrity**. Doing otherwise is pure mockery and hypocrisy. Opting for the other is placing the Order in disorder.

But what spells out our Rizalian integrity?

Sometimes the better way to understand a thing is recognizing what it is not.

Rizalian integrity is:

- Not about form, mediocrity and fashion but substance, excellence and passion
- Not rubbing elbows with those in power but engaging the minds and tapping the creative energies of doers
- Not about medals, ranks and positions but genuine commitment to the Rizalian ideals and principles
- Not punishing or killing the messenger and suppressing dissent but openly listening to the message and upholding free and open expression of ideas
- Not *palakasan* or *sistema padrino* but excellence, fairness, and being true to the Rizalian Knighthood of living genuinely *maginoo*.

Rizal was the epitome of dissent. And that is why he wrote and spoke and organized his fellow Filipinos. Any effort to mute dissent is locking Rizal back in his Fort Santiago cell. It is exiling him to Dapitan once more. It is marching him to Bagumbayan and executing him over and over and over again. Silencing dissent is undermining the spirit of Rizalism. And so we encourage dissent not for sentimental reasons, but because we cannot live without them.

Finally, given today's global realities, we need to look beyond the limited notion of nationalism and patriotism and work towards redeeming humanity.

Speaking at a Masonic Lodge *(La Solidaridad Lodge No. 53)* in Madrid in 1883, Rizal stressed:

> "The duty of modern man . . . is to work for the redemption of humanity. [And] humanity cannot be redeemed so long as there are oppressed peoples, so long as there are some men who live on the tears of many, so long as there are emasculated minds and blinded eyes that enable others to live like [rulers] who alone may enjoy beauty. Humanity cannot be redeemed while reason is not free, while faith would want to impose itself on facts, while whims are laws, and while there are nations who subjugate others."

These were words spoken 135 years ago but they still remain true today.

So let us take his enduring challenge of loving and fighting for our country, of redeeming humanity, and living with integrity. Anything less is an abdication of our social responsibility.

Aloha and mabuhay. Let's keep the Rizalian Spirit burning and alive. Have good day.

Delivered at the 7th USA Regional Assembly of the Knights of Rizal, Luxor Hotel, Las Vegas, August 31-September 2, 2018.

WHY ARE THE MOROS CONSPICUOUSLY ABSENT IN JOSE RIZAL'S WRITINGS?

Sir Federico V. Magdalena, PhD, KOR

FOR A MAN who has practically talked about every human group on earth, it comes as a big surprise why Dr. Jose Rizal is silent on the Moro people of Mindanao and Sulu.[1] He has not written about them in his voluminous writings, except tidbits (passing mention of places like Jolo, or its inhabitants) and a poem. The Moros are conspicuously absent in his writings. It appears though that he was aware of the Moro, judging from the information indicating his knowledge of the Moros, and the literature where he said little about them or the Muslims.

Yet, Rizal spoke of the great Arab writer Ibn Batuta in his correspondence with his Austrian friend, Ferdinand Blumentritt, and of the "little wars with the inhabitants of the South". Those inhabitants undoubtedly refer to the Moro as indigenous population of Mindanao.

He also engaged Don Vicente Barrantes in a literary debate for the latter's criticism of the *Noli Me Tangere*. Barrantes was the author of the famous book *Guerras piraticas de Filipinas* (1878), which talked about the piratical, dreaded Moros of Mindanao and Sulu that constantly attacked coastal towns in the Visayas and Luzon. Contemporary writers would pick up from this story and expanded their analysis. Rizal also annotated Antonio de Morga's book, *Sucesos de las Islas Filipinas* (1958), which chronicled numerous accounts of Spanish military expeditions against the Moros.

He also read and intended to publish Blumentritt's manuscript draft of the Ethnography of Mindanao, perhaps the single, most important writing on the peoples of the Philippines, including the Moros. A section in that book (trans. from German by Maceda, 1980:133-141) carries the title

"Pirate Groups of Mindanao and Sulu." There is also another section touching on the Moros under the geographic title as "Mindanao and the Sulu Archipelago" (Maceda, 1980: 169-173) whose interior remains "terra incognita." Rizal must have read the draft of Blumentritt's Ethnography manuscript as basis for this offer.

Rizal also wrote about a plan to send a group of Christian Filipinos as settlers or colonists in British North Borneo, ostensibly to establish a permanent community there (Reminiscences and Travels, 1961). It seems that this plan was submitted to North Borneo authorities, who were in-charge of the whole region after it was "ceded" (leased may be a better term) by the Sultan of Sulu to Baron Von Overbeck in 1778. Overbeck later turned over this territory to the British government, which relinquished it to the nascent Malaysian state. At that time, Rizal expected that the government of British North Borneo would grant the Filipino colony 5,000 acres or more, and possibly allocate 100,000 acres to be set aside for this colony to buy later. Nothing more was heard about this project, which could have settled the proprietary issue of the Moros in favor of the Philippines.

His knowledge of the Moros, or the place where they lived, was revealed in his correspondence with Dr. A. B. Meyer, who asked Rizal about Ibn Batuta, an Arab writer who used the place name "Tawalisi" if it meant the Philippines or a part of it.

Here, Rizal mentioned of Jolo, which may not be Batuta's Tawalisi. Rizal also mentioned of "women who fight like men. In the Filipino theater, a princess always appears with a warlike character, especially if she is a Moro woman" (Jose Rizal: Political and Historical Writings, 2011, p. 54). More importantly, Rizal lived in Mindanao during his four-year exile (1892-96) in Dapitan, now part of Zamboanga del Norte. There, he built houses to educate young boys and treat the sick, and taught the people of Dapitan modern ways of living. This sleepy village was a Subanen country, where this tribal group paid tribute to the Moro datus and recognized their authority. Datu Mandi of Zamboanga was one of the acknowledged Moro leaders in the area who exercised the power of taxation over the natives, including the Subanen of Dapitan and adjacent villages. Certainly, Rizal was aware of the situation of the tribal people, as some of his students were Subanen whose parents converted to Christianity.

How could Rizal have missed writing dedicatedly about the Moros, as he did to the women of Malolos for example? Or other essays like *Junto al Pasig* (Beside the Pasig River), *A La Juventud Filipina* (To the Filipino Youth), *La Indolencia de los Filipinos* (The Indolence of Filipinos) and *Kundiman* (Love song), among others. In his two famous novels, *Noli Me Tangere* and *El Filibusterismo*, none was said about a Moro character.

A probable explanation - or better yet, a hypothesis – is, that Rizal did not consider the Moros as part of *colonized* Philippines, hence they were NOT Filipinos unlike the rest of the Christianized natives. He must have also thought that the Philippines and its people were not yet a "nation," unlike the Moros who remained free and independent. The discussion below gives us some clue on this hypothesis.

In his correspondence with Blumentritt on December 30, 1886 on the meanings or differences between race, tribe and nation, Rizal said (Rizal-Blumentritt Correspondence, 1961, p. 33):

> "The races are the Caucasian, Mongolian, Malayan, and the black. We also give the name to a people of more than half a million souls that you call 'nations,' but we don't call 'nations' *peoples that are not independent* (italics are the author's); e.g., the Tagalog race, the Visayan, etc. But we say 'Spanish nation' instead of 'Spanish race.' Tribe is less than a race; it is part of race."

His reference to "more than half a million souls" are likely the Spanish categorization of *infieles*, or the American Non-Christian tribes (also Wards of the Nation), that include the Subanen of Dapitan and adjacent areas of Zamboanga. They, in contrast with the colonized natives (Tagalog, Visayan), were "nations" for being independent. The Tagalogs and Visayans were *not*.

Did Rizal consider the Moros a nation? That is, people who are independent and have their own political system? Following his statements above, it appears that he did, based on available information that they were, or could qualify as a "nation." Rizal knew that the Moros were governed by the sultanate or datuship. Definitely, he was aware of the fact that they lived outside the political influence of the Spanish government in Manila. Add to this the treaties that the Spanish government of the Philippines signed with the Moros until the 19th century.

Rizal was well read of events in the Philippines, and must have known of the relations between the Moros and the colonial government, including their conflict with Christian Filipinos as portrayed in the Moro-Moro or *zarzuela*. The latter did not escape his notice.

He could have known that a year before his exile in Dapitan, Spanish General Valeriano Weyler conducted military campaign in Lanao (1891). Years later, while Rizal was already in Dapitan, General Ramon Blanco laid siege to Marahui (now Marawi City) in 1895, destroyed the Moro fort and killed Ami Pakpak, acknowledged leader of the Maranao (Saber, 1980). Blanco and Rizal were acquaintances, both being Freemasons. In fact, it was Blanco who gave Rizal the permission to go to Cuba and also provided him safe passage for his travel from Dapitan to Manila to Spain.[2]

Rizal was no doubt familiar with the Moro's existence. His intimate view of them was reflected in one of three poems he wrote when he was younger, as a student at Ateneo. These poems suggest his knowledge of the history and culture of the Mindanao and Sulu Moros, and as well as those of the Muslims in Spain.

The closest that Rizal wrote dedicatedly about the Moros was revealed by his first poem entitled *El Combate: Urbiztondo, Terror de Jolo* (*The Battle: Urbiztondo, Terror of Jolo,* December 1875). Here, he praised Urbiztondo in his victorious battle with the Tausug in Jolo under Sultan Mahumat in 1851. He valorized the successful attack by Juan Antonio de Urbiztondo, who "spreads death everywhere, with cold steel in his hand."

Here's the last paragraph of the poem (translated in English):

> The fire consumes and devours
> The castles and palaces
> And all the Joloans own
> At our soldiers fierce attack.
> Perfidious Mahumat flees,
> Tyrannical and godless Sultan,
> And the warriors valorous
> March into Jolo as they sing.

Rizal's poem is a concoction of real and fictitious characters, or characterizations. Urbiztondo was the Spanish Governor-General of the Philippines at that time (1850-1853). But Sultan Mahumat appears to be fiction, as the Sultan of Sulu then was Sultan Pulalun Kiram (1844-1863), at times also called Mohammad Pulalun Kiram. The battle was real. It happened in 1850-1851, when Spanish forces attacked Tongkil Island (renamed Banguingi in modern times), and later besieged Jolo (Ang, no date) as a punitive expedition against the depredations of the Moros on Christian settlements in the Visayas and Luzon. As a consequence, the Sulu Sultan signed a treaty with the Philippine government under Urbiztondo for the "turning over" of his sovereignty. Some sources say, however, that the "turn over" was not mentioned in the Tausug text. Interesting story, with some twist.

In writing this poem, Rizal definitely got only the Spanish side of the story. The whole picture of the said attack was revealed 128 years later, in one of the many works of Warren (1978) who has studied the issue of piracy and trade in Sulu.

But then, we must remember that Rizal was a student at Ateneo, when he composed this poem two decades before his prime as a writer. At his youth, he seemed to identify with the Spanish in this war with the Moros (take note of "our soldiers" in the poem).

His other two poems were related, if tangentially, but not quite so for the Moros. Let us now turn to the second poem on the Muslims of Granada, Spain, titled *El Cautiverio y el Triunfo: Batalla de Lucena y Prision de Boabdil* (*Triumphant Entry of the Catholic Monarchs into Granada*, December 1876). The Muslims - or Moors - like the Sulu Moros, were also defeated by the rising Catholic kingdom under the conjugal rule of King Ferdinand II and Queen Isabella. Again, Rizal showed his admiration of the Spanish triumph over the "Mohammedans" as Granada fell in 1842. This shows that Rizal was reading world history even at a young age. He was said to be about 15 years old then.

Back to the "nation" argument. Spain was definitely a nation to Rizal's mind. He thought of the Spanish nation evolving, after King Ferdinand II took Spain from the hands of the Muslims who ruled over it for 700 years. Would he not consider the Moros of Mindanao and Sulu independent, for having been there for more than 400 years during his time? Or at least 100 years before the Spanish colonization of the Philippines?

Rizal was awed by the Spanish glory. No doubt, he proposed some reforms, one of which was to make *Las Islas Filipinas* (now Philippines) a province of Spain. The colonized islands were *not* a nation then. In fact, he imagined a country living under a sovereign state, Spain. Nevertheless, he placed the natives on a higher pedestal as *Indios bravos* (brave Indios, a counter to the derogatory term for natives).

Though the Moros were a nation, they did not seem to elicit much interest in his mind. Within the context of the Philippines, they were people who "did not belong" to Rizal's homeland.

The above statement has been the subject of the two-nation theory of peoplehood in India (i.e., Hindus and Muslims) before partition, which may apply to the Philippine case in reverse. It runs like this: in the Philippines, there reside two kinds of people: Bansang Filipino (Hispanized Filipinos, when the revolution broke out in 1896), and Bangsamoro (indigenous Moro nation).

IN CONCLUSION, tentative as it is always the case, we say that the Moros were conspicuously absent in Rizal's writings because he might have thought of them as a different people, or another nation. His writings thus focused on the Filipinos. The hypothesis we advanced earlier must have some truth in it.

Rizal also seemingly displayed lack of interest in the Moro people, due to the nature of Moro-Spanish, and Moro-Christian Filipino relations during his time. Together, these realities would explain the lack of space the Moros occupied in his vast repertoire of works, in stark contrast with that for other people or events, either in or outside of *Las Islas Filipinas*.

END NOTES

[1]In Spanish Philippines, the southern region where the Muslims were dominant was often referred to as "Mindanao and Sulu." Contemporary usage simply uses Mindanao to include all other island provinces like Sulu, Basilan and Tawi-Tawi.

[2]I am indebted to Sir Serafin (Jun) Colmenares, Jr. for sharing this information in an email correspondence, February 14, 2019.

BIBLIOGRAPHY

Ang, Josiah. "Historical of the Royal Sultanate of Sulu Including Related Events of Neighboring Peoples." In http://www.seasite.niu.edu/tagalog/modules/_modules/muslimmindanaohistorical_timeline_of_the_royal.htm.

Jose Rizal: Political and Historical Writings. Centennial Edition. Manila: Jose Rizal National Historical Commission of the Philippines, 2011. Maceda, Marcelino N. *An Attempt at Writing a Philippine Ethnography by Ferdinand Blumentritt.* Trans. from the original German text. Marawi City: University Research Center, Mindanao State University, 1980.

Morga, Antonio de. *Sucesos de las Islas Filipinas.* Por el doctor Antonio de Mora, con anotaciones del Dr. Jose Rizal. Quezon City: R. Martinez, 1958.

Reminiscences and Travels of Jose Rizal. Manila: National Historical Commission, 1961.

Rizal-Blumentritt Correspondence, a Centennial Edition. Manila: Jose Rizal National Centennial Commission, 1961.

Rizal, Jose. *The Battle: Urbiztondo, Terror of Jolo (El Combate: Urbiztondo, Terror de Jolo),* December 1875). Poem, in https://happyschool.com/philippine-studies/jose-rizal's-poems-compilation.

Rizal, Jose. *The Captivity and the Triumph: Battle of Lucena and the Imprisonment of Boabdil (El Cautiverio y el Triunfo: Batalla de Lucena y Prision de Boabdil),* December 1876. Poem, in https://happyschool.com/philippine-studies/jose-rizal's-poems-compilation.

Saber, Mamitua. *The Battle of Marawi, 1895, and Other Essays.* Marawi City: University Research Center, 1980.

Warren, Jim. "Who were the Balangingi Samal? Slave Raiding and Ethnogenesis in Nineteenth-Century Sulu." *Journal of Asian Studies,* Vol. 37, No. 3 (May, 1978), pp. 477-490. Available at: http://www.jstor.org/stable/2053573.

RIZAL'S LEGACY: LOVE OF GOD AND TENACITY

Sir Tom D. Rodriguez, LL.B, KGCR

GOOD AFTERNOON, Brother Knights and Ladies for Rizal.

When you hear the word legacy, you probably think of what you will leave behind or how you will be remembered when you are gone.

Someone on the Internet had asked the question, "Was Jose Rizal an atheist?" Somebody answered the question by stating that "most historians regard Rizal as an atheist." However, she did not mention the names of these historians who considered Rizal as an atheist. Who among you considers Rizal an atheist?

This afternoon, I submit to you that Rizal believed in God and left a legacy of the Love of God. You may ask, how did Dr. Rizal accomplish living a legacy of love of God? How can we prove that Rizal loved God?

We can prove it not only by his own writings but also by his deeds, the way he acted in accordance with the Holy Scriptures. Rizal gave us some principles to live by, namely:

- He taught us to be thankful to God and not to worry about anything because we are all in the hands of the Divine Providence.

- He taught us to be forgiving; that God is merciful and, therefore, we should also be merciful.

- He taught us that education without God is not true education.

- He admonished us to teach our children acts of honesty and deed, love for the fellowman, and respect for God.

How do we know that Rizal was thankful to God?

Rizal had offered his services as a military doctor in Cuba, which was then in the throes of a revolution and a raging yellow fever epidemic. There was a shortage of physicians to minister to the needs of the Spanish troops and the Cuban people.[1] On September 2, 1896, the day before his departure for Spain, on his way to Cuba, Rizal, on board the *Castilla*, wrote to his mother, and I quote in part:

> My Dearest Mother,
> Xxx
>
> I am well, *thank God*: I am only concerned as to what will happen or shall have happened to you in these days of upheaval and disorder. *God will* that my old father may not have any indisposition. Xxx *Do not worry about anything, we are all in the hands of the Divine Providence.* Not all those who go to Cuba die, and in the end, one has to die; at least die doing something good. Xxx A fond embrace for every one of my sisters; may they love one another just as I love all of them.
>
> Your son, Jose.[2]

Rizal taught us to be forgiving and be merciful.

On December 29, 1896, the eve before his execution, Rizal informed Captain Dominguez who was with him that he *forgave his enemies,* including the military judges who condemned him to death,[3] echoing the words of Jesus on the cross, "Father, forgive them, for they do not know what they are doing." (Luke 23:34).

When Rizal was in Brussels, he received bad news from home in Calamba, Laguna. The Dominican Order continually raised the land rents until such time that Rizal's father refused to pay his rent. Other tenants, inspired by Don Francisco's courage, also refused to pay the unreasonable rents. The tenants, including the Rizal family, were persecuted. Paciano and the brothers-in-law Antonio Lopez (husband of

Narcisa) and Silvestre Ubaldo (husband of Olympia) were deported to Mindoro. Another brother-in-law, Manuel T. Hidalgo (husband of Saturnina) was banished for a second time to Bohol.

The sad news from home depressed Rizal. His heart bled to know the sorrowful plight of his parents, brother, and brothers-in-law. From Brussels, he wrote to his sister Soledad on June 6, 1890:

> xxx I may be what my enemies desire me to be, yet never an accusation are they able to hurl against me which makes me blush or lower my forehead and I hope *that God will be merciful enough with me* to prevent me from committing one of those faults which would involve my family."[4]

Rizal invoked the mercy of God that would prevent him from committing vengeance against his enemies. Jesus on the Sermon on the Mount said, "Blessed are the merciful for they shall be shown mercy." (Matthew 5:7)

Rizal taught us that education without God is not true education.

Dr. Rizal said that proper education is the key to freedom from poverty and ignorance. Rizal also expressed his belief in the supreme importance of religion in the education of man. In his poem, "Intimate Alliance Between Religion and Education," he said that education without God is not true education.[5]

Rizal believed in God. He never denied the existence of God or the role of a Supreme Being in his life. In fact, Rizal had a healthy, fresh and perceptive idea of divinity. The leader who believes in a Supreme Being, a personal God, has a greater capacity to endure, to hope, to persevere and even to be happy.[6]

As a Christian humanist, Rizal believed that man was created by God in his own image and was "endowed with reason and will of his own.[7]

One has said that Rizal was never anti-God or anti-church. He was anti-cleric to those who abused their duty and concealed behind their conceited robe of religiosity. He knew there were those who practiced religion but do not worship God.[7]

According to Rizal, individual judgment is *a gift from God* and everybody should use it like a lantern to show the way and that self-esteem, if moderated by judgment, saves man from unworthy acts.[8]

Rizal wants us to teach our children honesty, love for our fellowman, and respect for God.

While in London, Rizal wrote to the young women of Malolos, Bulacan, on Feb. 22, 1889. The story behind this letter was that a group of 21 young women in Malolos wanted to set up a night school, at their own expense, where they could learn the Spanish language. The parish priest, Fray Garcia, turned down their request, apparently for fears that such would open them up to progressive or some seditious ideas from abroad.

The young women appealed to Governor General Valeriano Weyler with a petition to allow the establishment of the night school where they could attend Spanish classes, accompanied by their respective mothers. The governor acceded to their request, and the news of the Malolos women reached Rizal, who was inspired to write a letter to enjoin them to be the pride of country, to love God and instill the same virtues to their children.

Rizal said, "Let us be reasonable and open our eyes, especially you women, because you are the first to influence the consciousness of man. Remember that a good mother does not resemble the mother that the friar has created; she must bring up her child to be the *image of a God who is the father of us all*, who is just; x x x Awaken and prepare the will of our children towards all that is honorable, judged by proper standards, to all that is sincere and firm of purpose, clear judgment, clear procedure, *honesty in act and deed, love for the fellowman and respect for God; this is what you must teach your children.*[9] He further wrote: "Saintliness consists, in the first place, in obeying the dictates of reason, happen what may."

"It is acts and not words that I want of you," said Christ. "Not everyone that sayeth unto me, 'Lord, Lord' shall enter into the kingdom of heaven; but he that doeth the will of my Father which is in Heaven. xxx Blessed be they who gives assistance to their fellowmen, aid the poor, and feed the hungry; but cursed be they who turn a deaf ear to the supplications of the poor . . . .[10]

Although Rizal did not give a specific verse when he wrote this to the young women of Malolos, he was referring to Matthew 7:21 when Jesus taught about those who build their houses on Rock and Sand (See also Luke 6:46-49). Matthew 7:24-27 says: "Therefore, everyone who hears these words of mine and puts them into practice is like a wise man who built his house on the rock. The rain came down, the streams rose, and the winds blew and beat against that house; yet it did not fall, because it had its foundation on the rock. But everyone who hears these words of mine and does not put them into practice is like a foolish man who built his house on sand. The rain came down, the streams rose, and the winds blew and beat against that house, and it fell with a great crash."

What Rizal taught, he practiced it. Rizal practiced medicine in Dapitan. He had many patients, but most of them were poor so that he even gave them free medicine.[11] In his letter to Blumentritt on March 13, Rizal said that he had 16 pupils in his school and that these pupils did not pay any tuition. Instead of charging them tuition fees, he made them work in his garden, fields, and construction projects in the community.[12]

When Rizal arrived in Dapitan, he decided to improve the town, to the best of his God-given talents, and to awaken the civic consciousness of the people. Aside from constructing Dapitan's first water system, he spent months draining the marshes in order to get rid of malaria that infested the town.[13]

Jesus said, "whatever you did for one of the least of these brothers of mine, you did for me." (Matthew 25: 40) Again, I ask you, how do we know that Rizal loved God?

First, in his "Last Farewell," he said, "I shall be where no slaves bow to a master; where faith does not kill and *where God is the only one Supreme."*

Second, at 5:30 a.m., Rizal embraced Josephine Bracken for the last time, and gave her a last gift – a religious book, *Imitation of Christ*, by Father Thomas à Kempis, which he autographed: "To my dear unhappy wife, Josephine. December 30th, 1896 – Jose Rizal."[14]

Third, the last words of Rizal were *"Consummatum est*! It is finished – the same words that Jesus had uttered before he died on the cross. (John 19:30)

Dr. Rizal revered God. Our heroes, like Rizal, are fearless people who take on all dangers and overcome them. The Book of Life teaches us that fear of God can lead to a fearless life. To fear God means to respect and revere him as the Almighty Lord. When we trust God completely to take care of us, we will find that our fears – even death itself – will subside. No wonder, Dr. Rizal was found by the physician who examined him to have a normal pulse just before he was shot by a firing squad. He became fearless – even before death itself because he trusted God completely.

Fourth, in Rizal's poem entitled, "Youth," he said:

> Raise your children close to the image of the true God –

The God who cannot be bribed
The God who is not avaricious
The God who is the father of all,
Who is not partial,
The God who does not fatten on the food of the poor,
Who does not rejoice at the plants of the affected
And does not obfuscate the intelligent mind.
Awaken and prepare the mind of the child
For every good and desirable idea –
Love for honor, sincere and firm character,
Clear mind, clean conduct, noble action.
Love for one's fellowmen, respect for God –
Teach this to your children.[15]

Fifth, Rizal's first novel, *Noli Me Tangere*, is a Latin phrase which means "Touch Me Not." It is not originally conceived by Rizal, as he admitted taking it from the Bible. The biblical source was the Gospel of St. John (Chapter 20, Verses 13 to 17). According to St. John, on the First Easter Sunday, St. Mary Magdalene visited the Holy Sepulcher, and to her Jesus, just arisen from the dead, said:

> "Touch me not; I am not yet ascended to my Father, but go to my brethren, and say unto them I am ascending to my Father and your Father; and to my God and your God."[16]

Jose Rizal did have faith in God. Rizal strongly believed that God guides the destiny of all nations and men. He also believed that someday all men would have to answer for their deeds on earth to a just and strict God.[17]

Rizal was the first leader in Asia to maintain that each person possessed inalienable, inviolable rights, belonging to him *because they were granted by God his creator,* which could not be trampled down or taken away from the individual without violating God's purpose.[18]

On 9 October 1896, Rizal was again returning to the Philippines after being placed under arrest while on his way to serve as a volunteer doctor for the Spanish army fighting Cuban rebels. Calmly, Rizal wrote in his diary: *"May God's will always be done...*Oh Lord, Thou art my hope, my consolation! Thy will be done, and I am only too ready to obey it."[19]

Rizal gave his life to free us from the bondage of oppression and despotism, while Jesus Christ gave his life to free us from the bondage to sin.

And we rejoice in the hope of the glory of God. Not only so, but we also rejoice in our sufferings, because we know that suffering produces perseverance; perseverance, character; and character hope. And hope does not disappoint us, because God has poured out his love into our hearts by the Holy Spirit, whom he has given us. (Roman 5:2-5) [NIV].

NOT ONLY DID RIZAL LEAVE a legacy of the Love of God but also the virtue of tenacity or perseverance.

Here is an example of Rizal showing tenacity or perseverance. In the reunion of Filipinos in the Paterno residence in Madrid on January 2, 1884, Rizal proposed the writing of a novel about the Philippines by a group of Filipinos. His proposal was unanimously approved by those present, among whom were the Paternos (Pedro, Maximo and Antonio), Graciano Lopez Jaena, Evaristo Aguirre, Eduardo de Lete, Julio Lorente, Melecio Figueroa, and Valentin Ventura.

Unfortunately, Rizal's project did not materialize. Those compatriots who were expected to collaborate on the novel did not write anything. The novel was designed to cover all phases of Philippine life. However, almost everybody wanted to write on women. Rizal was disgusted at such flippancy. He was more disgusted to see that his companions, instead of working seriously on the novel, wasted their time gambling or flirting with Spanish señoritas.

Undaunted by his friend's indifference, he is determined to write the novel alone.[20]

The friends of Rizal hailed the novel, praising it in glowing colors. As to be expected, Rizal's enemies condemned it. Rizal anticipated the vitriolic attacks of his enemies, who were sore to be told the truth of their evil ways. As he told Blumentritt: "The government and the friars will probably attack the work, refuting my statements, but *I trust in the God of truth* and in persons who have actually seen our sufferings.[21]

After Rizal wrote the *Noli*, letters from home hinted that his family was beginning to suffer the consequences of his novel. Although Rizal was not personally intimidated, the threat posed to his parents was another matter. He announced that he was coming home to face the consequences of his actions. Friends and relatives begged him not to return to the Philippines. But Rizal could be as stubborn as his mother when he chose to be. And nothing could change his mind. One letter to his family ended on this fatalistic note: "Into your hands, Lord, I commend my spirit."[22] You may recognize that prayer was the same as Jesus's final cry from the cross. By praying that word in the moments before his death, Jesus demonstrated His intimate relationship with the Father and pointed believers toward their home with Him. (John 14:3)

So, what can we learn from Rizal as a model? He stuck to his mission. Rizal knew his mission, and he did not deviate from it. Rizal had no ambivalence about who he was or what he was supposed to do. He showed the virtue of tenacity.

Now that we are reminded Rizal taught us to be forgiving – that God is merciful and therefore we should also be merciful, should we as Knights of Rizal and Ladies for Rizal be like Rizal and Jesus who forgave even those who put them to death?

Rizal not only admonished us as Knights but also urged us to teach our children honesty, love for our fellowman, and respect for God. I know that we will learn something out of this assembly, and I hope among them are Love of God and honesty in words and in deed.

Our words lack meaning if our actions do not back them up. We can say we love God or others, but if we are not taking practical steps to demonstrate that love, our words are empty and meaningless. How well do our actions back up what we say?

Shall we build our house of principles like a wise man who builds it on a rock-foundation or a foolish man who builds it on sand? The answer is yours.

Rizal's love of God and tenacity will resonate within our society, in the world today, tomorrow and years to come. Thank you and God bless everyone.

NOTE: Emphases (*italizations*) in this article are the author's.

End Notes

1 Gregorio F. Zaide and Sonia M. Zaide, *Jose Rizal Life, Works, and Writings of a Genius, Writer, Scientist, and National Hero*, 2nd edition, All Nations Publishing Co., Quezon City, Philippines, p. 240-241
2 Zaide, p. 246- 247
3 Zaide, p. 265.
4 Zaide, p. 171
5 Rizal's Ideas/Thoughts/Views on Government and Education. Castillo, Mario L., P. 46.
6 P. 55. Almonte, Napoleon. Rizal is My President. Impress Quality Printing Phils. Inc., 2009.)
7 Lizardo, Fidela S. Nationalist Ideas of Rizal, quoted in Remembering Rizal – A Compilation of Literary Works about Dr. Jose P. Rizal by different Authors. B.S. Lizardo Enterprise Publishing, 2004, Caloocan City, P. 29. Lizardo, etc.
7a "The Controversy of Philippine National Hero (Dr. Jose Rizal) – The Story." Internet.
8 Zaide, p. 221.
9 Zaide, p. 327
10 Zaide p.326.
11 Zaide, p. 229.

12 Zaide, p. 267.

13 Zaide, p. 228.

14 Boquiren, Modesta G., "Poems for Filipino Children, Youth, p. 209, quoted p. 12 "Remembering Rizal, Fidela S. Lizardo and Bernardita S. Lizardo. B.S. Lizardo Enterprise, 2005.

15 Zaide, p. 327

16 Zaide, p. 91-92.

17 Lizardo, p. 28

18 Lizardo, p. 29

19 Trillana, Pablo III, "Rizal: The Tagalog Christ", quoted in *Rizal and Heroic Traditions: A Sense of National Destiny*, New Day Publishers, 2005, p. 40.

20 Palma, Rafael, *The Pride of the Malay Race*, Prentice-Hall, New York, 1949, p. 262-262.

21 Zaide, p. 88-89.

22 Zaide, p. 188.

23   Bantug, Asuncion Lopez-Rizal, *Indio Bravo - The Story of Jose Rizal*, Tahanan Books, Makati, p. 71-72.

Epilogue

ACROSS THE GLOBE, the first quarter of the 21st century is witnessing both sides of the reality spectrum – hope and despair, progress and regression, freedom and suppression. While science and technology have significantly advanced, some outmoded elements of the social structure have remained intact. Wealth may have exponentially multiplied but poverty and inequity continue to hold back sectors of society that have been historically ignored and neglected. People may now be more aware of their rights but violation of the same is on the rise, remaining to be a great concern. Discrimination, bigotry and the distorted sense of superiority and entitlement continue to deny others of equal treatment. Corruption, plunder, and abuse of power are familiar affairs in government, effectively eroding public trust in the system. The break of dawn may be at hand but patches of thick clouds continue to hover on the horizon, trying to keep the new day in darkness.

This is why a glow in the dark remains relevant even in our present time. That glow offers us a reason to still hope for a promising day – the hope in the restoration of our faith in human capacities and in the goodness of humankind. And we may glean this hope from the life, ideals and works of men and women who have come before us – or live among us – and stood righteously and courageously to rekindle the fading light.

Dr. Jose Rizal is certainly among those figures who offers such hope and inspiration for all ages, particularly the young generation. Not only was he one of the greatest intellectuals of his time; he was and is a model for non-violent change, complimenting peace advocates like Mahatma Gandhi, Dr. Martin Luther King, Jr., Nelson Mandela, and Malala

Yousafzai, among others. As he once wrote, "not all were asleep during the night of our forefathers." There were those who spent long and trying vigils to defend freedom and human dignity, some of them – including Rizal himself – giving up their lives for such cause.

Rizal is an enduring social conscience and an unwavering moral compass even in contemporary times. We will continue to read, hear and talk about about him as his teachings are timeless and his life was inspiring. He remains to be a spark, a glow, and a flame that will lend light to the global society repeatedly threatened by crisis and darkness.

Sir Serafin P. Colmenares, Jr., PhD, KGCR
Sir Raymund Ll. Liongson, PhD, KGCR
Editors

About the Authors

Patricio "Jojo" N. Abinales, PhD, is currently professor at the School for Pacific and Asian Studies, University of Hawaii-Manoa. Prior to joining the University of Hawaii in 2011, Jojo taught at the Department of Political Science at Ohio University from 1997 to 1999 before moving to the Center for Southeast Asian Studies at Kyoto University in 2000. He was a visiting scholar at the Woodrow Wilson International Center for Scholars in Washington DC in 2010-2011. Among his publications are *State and Society in the Philippines* (2005, 2017) which he co-authored with his late wife Donna J. Amoroso, and *Orthodoxy and History in the Muslim Mindanao Narrative* (2010). Jojo obtained his B.A. in History from the University of the Philippines-Diliman and his Ph.D. in Government and Asian Studies from Cornell University.

Belinda "Lindy"A. Aquino, PhD, professor emeritus of Political Science and Asian Studies, is an internationally recognized authority on contemporary Philippine affairs. She established and was the first Director of the Center for Philippine Studies at the University of Hawaii at Manoa. She was vice president for public affairs of the University of the Philippines in 1989-1991. Lindy obtained her Ph.D. in government (political science) from Cornell University, her M.A. in political science from the University of Hawaii at Manoa, and her B.A. degree in English from the University of the Philippines at Diliman. She is the author of *Politics of Plunder: The Philippines Under Marcos* (1987). Lindy was the first recipient of the Dr. Jose P. Rizal Award for Peace and Social Justice from the Knights of Rizal-Hawaii Chapter in 2011.

Clement "Clem" Bautista, MA, KGOR, is the director of the Office of Multicultural Student Services at the University of Hawaii at Manoa. He holds a bachelor's degree in anthropology and a master's degree in public policy from the University of Chicago and has pursued graduate studies in sociology and Southeast Asian history and philosophy at the University of Hawaii at Manoa. He was the administrator of *e*Fil: Filipino Digital Archives and History Center of Hawaii (efilarchives.org/), an online resource about Filipinos and the Filipino experience in Hawaii. Clem is a member of the Board of Directors of the Filipino Community Center, past president of the Filipino-American Historical Society of Hawaii, and a past commander of the Knights of Rizal-Hawaii Chapter. He wrote *[Un]-Boxing Rizal's Legacy* (2013).

Virgie Chattergy, EdD, is professor emeritus at the University of Hawaii at Manoa, College of Education. She obtained her BSE-Ed degree from St. Theresa's College in Cebu, Philippines and her Ed.D. and a Certificate in Teaching English as a Second Language from the University of California, Los Angeles. Over the years, Dr. Chattergy has assumed various roles, ranging from professor to director of faculty development and academic support services to assistant dean of the Office of Student Academic Services. A recipient of various grants and awards, she co-authored the book The Ethics of Multicultural and Bilingual Education (1992) and wrote the article Being a Teacher in a Multicultural Classroom (1993) among others. Her latest publication, co-authored with Pepi Nieva, is a collection of stories by Filipino women entitled *Pinay: Culture Bearers of the Filipino Diaspora* (2017).

Serafin "Jun" P. Colmenares Jr., PhD, KGCR, is administrator of the Hawaii State Health Planning & Development Agency and previously served as the first executive director of the Hawaii Office of Language Access. He was a professor at the Mindanao State University in the Philippines before coming to Hawaii in 1988. Jun has co-authored the book *Bold Dream, Uncommon Valor: The Florentino Das Story* (2012) and co-edited *Jose Rizal's Legacy and Nation Building* (2013). A past chapter, area and

USA deputy regional commander, he is currently commander of the Knights of Rizal-Aloha Chapter. Jun holds an MPH degree from the University of Hawaii, M.A. and Ph.D. degrees in political science from the University of Delhi in India, and a bachelor's degree in political science from the Mindanao State University.

Patricia "Pat" Espiritu-Halagao, PhD, is professor and chair of the Department of Curriculum Studies at the University of Hawaii at Manoa, College of Education. Her scholarship focuses on social studies and multicultural education, specifically Filipinos in K-12 education. She received the Board of Regents Medal for Excellence in Teaching (2012). She served on the Hawai'i State Board of Education (2013-2016), championing equity and cultural & linguistic policies on multilingualism and the Seal of Biliteracy. She is co-author of *Bold Dream, Uncommon Valor: The Florentino Das Story* (2012). Pat received her Ph.D. degree in Education and her M.Ed. from the University of Washington, her teaching credential from San Francisco State University, as well as her B.A. in Anthropology from Occidental College.

Raymund Ll. Liongson, PhD, KGCR, is a retired professor and coordinator of the Philippine Studies program at the University of Hawaii-Leeward Community College. He obtained his Ph.D. in Education from the University of the Philippines at Diliman. Raymund is co-editor of *Jose Rizal's Legacy and Nation Building* (2013), *Essays in Ilokano and Amianan Life, Language and Literature* (2006), *Saritaan ken Sukisok: Discourse and Research in Ilokano Language, Culture and Politics* (2006) and has authored several articles on Philippine history and politics and civil/ human rights. He was a member of the Hawaii Civil Rights Commission, past president of the Filipino Coalition for Solidarity and past board member of the Filipino Community Center. A past commander of the KOR Hawaii Chapter, he is currently Pursuivant of the Aloha Chapter and area commander (Western USA-Hawaii) of the Knights of

Rizal. In 2011, Raymund was recognized as a Distinguished Alumnus of the University of the Philippines.

Federico "Fred" V. Magdalena, PhD, KOR, is currently faculty specialist at the Center for Philippine Studies and a faculty affiliate at the University of Hawaii at Manoa Asian Studies Program. His research specializations are on Mindanao, Islam, Philippine society and culture, and globalization of cultures. Among his publications are: 'Dabao-kuo and the Winning of Mindanao" (2009); *The Battle of Bayang and Other Essays on Moroland* (2002); and "The Chinese in Moroland" (2001). Fred obtained his Ph.D. degree in sociology from the University of Hawaii at Manoa, his M.A. from the University of the Philippines at Diliman, and his B.A. from the Mindanao State University. He currently serves as archivist of the Knights of Rizal-Aloha Chapter.

Floro C. Quibuyen, PhD, KCR, is a retired associate professor of Philippine Studies at the Asian Center of the University of the Philippines. He holds a Ph.D. in Political Science and M.A in Anthropology from the University of Hawaii at Manoa, a B.A in Philosophy from the University of the Philippines at Diliman, and a Diploma in Community Services Work from the BCA National Training Group, Sydney. Floro taught for 29 years at the University of Hawaii at Manoa, University of the Philippines at Diliman, and the University of Santo Tomas. His publications on Rizal and Philippine history include *A Nation Aborted: Rizal, American Hegemony and Philippine Nationalism* (2008) and *"and woman will prevail over man": Symbolic Sexual Inversion and Counter-Hegemonic Discourse in Mt. Banahaw* (1991).

Eva Washburn-Repollo, PhD, is an associate professor at Chaminade University. She received her bachelor's degree in speech and theater arts, as well as her master's degree in literature, from Silliman University in the Philippines. She also obtained her master's degree in reading from Southern Connecticut State University and her Ph.D. degree from the

University of Hawaii at Manoa. Eva has written and directed three documentaries focused on the values of multicultural selves in a diverse learning environment. She also contributed a chapter on multilingualism, whiteness and anxieties of whiteness, and the sociological environmental dimension of development, to the book *Whiteness Interrogated.* She currently serves as a commissioner on the Hawaii State Foundation on Culture and the Arts.

Tom "Judge Tom" D. Rodriguez, LLB, KGCR is former supervising administrative law judge for the State of New York. Known as "the singing judge," Judge Tom graduated from the University of the Philippines College of Law (1963) and went into private practice while serving as an associate editor of two legal publications" the *Philippine Law Decisions* and the *Philippine Tax Journal.* He passed the New York State Bar and became an associate litigation attorney for the Wall Street law firm Curtis-Mallet Prevost Colt & Mosle. He is the author of *Practical Guide: Procedures in Opening a New Business in New York* (1981). Judge Tom was formerly commander of the New York Chapter, past area commander and past USA Regional Commander of the Knights of Rizal.

Elihu A. Ybañez, LLB, KGCR is currently an associate justice of the Philippine Court of Appeals. He obtained his B.A. in political science from Philippine Christian University and his law degree from San Beda College of Law. He also has a master's degree in National Security Administration from the National Defense College of the Philippines and is a graduate of the Command and General Staff College in Fort Bonifacio. He first served in the Office of the Solicitor General, then joined the judiciary as presiding and then executive judge of the Regional Trial Court in Batangas before his appointment as associate justice. Elihu is a Brigadier General of the Reserved Force of the Armed Forces of the Philippines and was Wing Commander in the 1st Air Force Wing Reserve, National Capital Region. Justice Ybañez is currently the Supreme Commander of the Knights of Rizal.

INDEX

www.ingramcontent.com/pod-product-compliance
Lightning Source LLC
Chambersburg PA
CBHW070804240726
48654CB00007B/207